The Federal Aviation Administration

The Federal Aviation Administration

Robert Burkhardt

CHELSEA HOUSE PUBLISHERS

Chelsea House Publishers

Editor-in-Chief: Nancy Toff
Executive Editor: Remmel T. Nunn
Managing Editor: Karyn Gullen Browne
Copy Chief: Juliann Barbato
Picture Editor: Adrian G. Allen
Art Director: Maria Epes
Manufacturing Manager: Gerald Levine

Know Your Government

Senior Editor: Kathy Kuhtz

Staff for THE FEDERAL AVIATION ADMINISTRATION

Deputy Copy Chief: Ellen Scordato
Editorial Assistant: Elizabeth Nix
Picture Coordinator: Michèle Brisson
Picture Research: Dixon & Turner Research Associates, Inc.
Assistant Art Director: Laurie Jewell
Senior Designer: Noreen M. Lamb
Layout: Arlene Goldberg
Production Coordinator: Joseph Romano

First Printing

1 3 5 7 9 8 6 4 2

Library of Congress Cataloging-in-Publication Data

Burkhardt, Robert.
   The Federal Aviation Administration.
   (Know your government)
   Bibliography: p.
   Includes index.
   1. United States. Federal Aviation Administration.   2. Aeronautics, Commercial—
Government policy—United States.   I. Title. II. Series: Know your government (New York,
N.Y.)
HE9803.A35B87   1989   353.0087'77   88-25746
ISBN 1-55546-107-7
      0-7910-0863-0 (pbk.)

CONTENTS

KNOW YOUR GOVERNMENT

THE AMERICAN RED CROSS

THE BUREAU OF INDIAN AFFAIRS

THE CENTRAL INTELLIGENCE AGENCY

THE COMMISSION ON CIVIL RIGHTS

THE DEPARTMENT OF AGRICULTURE

THE DEPARTMENT OF THE AIR FORCE

THE DEPARTMENT OF THE ARMY

THE DEPARTMENT OF COMMERCE

THE DEPARTMENT OF DEFENSE

THE DEPARTMENT OF EDUCATION

THE DEPARTMENT OF ENERGY

THE DEPARTMENT OF HEALTH AND HUMAN SERVICES

THE DEPARTMENT OF HOUSING AND URBAN DEVELOPMENT

THE DEPARTMENT OF THE INTERIOR

THE DEPARTMENT OF JUSTICE

THE DEPARTMENT OF LABOR

THE DEPARTMENT OF THE NAVY

THE DEPARTMENT OF STATE

THE DEPARTMENT OF TRANSPORTATION

THE DEPARTMENT OF THE TREASURY

THE DRUG ENFORCEMENT ADMINISTRATION

THE ENVIRONMENTAL PROTECTION AGENCY

THE EQUAL EMPLOYMENT OPPORTUNITIES COMMISSION

THE FEDERAL AVIATION ADMINISTRATION

THE FEDERAL BUREAU OF INVESTIGATION

THE FEDERAL COMMUNICATIONS COMMISSION

THE FEDERAL GOVERNMENT: HOW IT WORKS

THE FEDERAL RESERVE SYSTEM

THE FEDERAL TRADE COMMISSION

THE FOOD AND DRUG ADMINISTRATION

THE FOREST SERVICE

THE HOUSE OF REPRESENTATIVES

THE IMMIGRATION AND NATURALIZATION SERVICE

THE INTERNAL REVENUE SERVICE

THE LIBRARY OF CONGRESS

THE NATIONAL AERONAUTICS AND SPACE ADMINISTRATION

THE NATIONAL ARCHIVES AND RECORDS ADMINISTRATION

THE NATIONAL FOUNDATION ON THE ARTS AND HUMANITIES

THE NATIONAL PARK SERVICE

THE NATIONAL SCIENCE FOUNDATION

THE NUCLEAR REGULATORY COMMISSION

THE PEACE CORPS

THE PRESIDENCY

THE PUBLIC HEALTH SERVICE

THE SECURITIES AND EXCHANGE COMMISSION

THE SENATE

THE SMALL BUSINESS ADMINISTRATION

THE SMITHSONIAN

THE SUPREME COURT

THE TENNESSEE VALLEY AUTHORITY

THE U.S. ARMS CONTROL AND DISARMAMENT AGENCY

THE U.S. COAST GUARD

THE U.S. CONSTITUTION

THE U.S. FISH AND WILDLIFE SERVICE

THE U.S. INFORMATION AGENCY

THE U.S. MARINE CORPS

THE U.S. MINT

THE U.S. POSTAL SERVICE

THE U.S. SECRET SERVICE

THE VETERANS ADMINISTRATION

CHELSEA HOUSE PUBLISHERS

Government: Crises of Confidence

Arthur M. Schlesinger, jr.

From the start, Americans have regarded their government with a mixture of reliance and mistrust. The men who founded the republic did not doubt the indispensability of government. "If men were angels," observed the 51st Federalist Paper, "no government would be necessary." But men are not angels. Because human beings are subject to wicked as well as to noble impulses, government was deemed essential to assure freedom and order.

At the same time, the American revolutionaries knew that government could also become a source of injury and oppression. The men who gathered in Philadelphia in 1787 to write the Constitution therefore had two purposes in mind. They wanted to establish a strong central authority and to limit that central authority's capacity to abuse its power.

To prevent the abuse of power, the Founding Fathers wrote two basic principles into the new Constitution. The principle of federalism divided power between the state governments and the central authority. The principle of the separation of powers subdivided the central authority itself into three branches—the executive, the legislative, and the judiciary—so that "each may be a check on the other." The *Know Your Government* series focuses on the major executive departments and agencies in these branches of the federal government.

7

The Constitution did not plan the executive branch in any detail. After vesting the executive power in the president, it assumed the existence of "executive departments" without specifying what these departments should be. Congress began defining their functions in 1789 by creating the Departments of State, Treasury, and War. The secretaries in charge of these departments made up President Washington's first cabinet. Congress also provided for a legal officer, and President Washington soon invited the attorney general, as he was called, to attend cabinet meetings. As need required, Congress created more executive departments.

Setting up the cabinet was only the first step in organizing the American state. With almost no guidance from the Constitution, President Washington, seconded by Alexander Hamilton, his brilliant secretary of the treasury, equipped the infant republic with a working administrative structure. The Federalists believed in both executive energy and executive accountability and set high standards for public appointments. The Jeffersonian opposition had less faith in strong government and preferred local government to the central authority. But when Jefferson himself became president in 1801, although he set out to change the direction of policy, he found no reason to alter the framework the Federalists had erected.

By 1801 there were about 3,000 federal civilian employees in a nation of a little more than 5 million people. Growth in territory and population steadily enlarged national responsibilities. Thirty years later, when Jackson was president, there were more than 11,000 government workers in a nation of 13 million. The federal establishment was increasing at a faster rate than the population.

Jackson's presidency brought significant changes in the federal service. He believed that the executive branch contained too many officials who saw their jobs as "species of property" and as "a means of promoting individual interest." Against the idea of a permanent service based on life tenure, Jackson argued for the periodic redistribution of federal offices, contending that this was the democratic way and that official duties could be made "so plain and simple that men of intelligence may readily qualify themselves for their performance." He called this policy rotation-in-office. His opponents called it the spoils system.

In fact, partisan legend exaggerated the extent of Jackson's removals. More than 80 percent of federal officeholders retained their jobs. Jackson discharged no larger a proportion of government workers than Jefferson had done a generation earlier. But the rise in these years of mass political parties gave federal patronage new importance as a means of building the party and of rewarding activists. Jackson's successors were less restrained in the distribution of spoils. As the federal establishment grew—to nearly 40,000 by 1861—the politicization of the public service excited increasing concern.

After the Civil War the spoils system became a major political issue. High-minded men condemned it as the root of all political evil. The spoilsmen, said the British commentator James Bryce, "have distorted and depraved the mechanism of politics." Patronage, by giving jobs to unqualified, incompetent, and dishonest persons, lowered the standards of public service and nourished corrupt political machines. Office-seekers pursued presidents and cabinet secretaries without mercy. "Patronage," said Ulysses S. Grant after his presidency, "is the bane of the presidential office." "Every time I appoint someone to office," said another political leader, "I make a hundred enemies and one ingrate." George William Curtis, the president of the National Civil Service Reform League, summed up the indictment. He said,

> The theory which perverts public trusts into party spoils, making public
> employment dependent upon personal favor and not on proved merit,
> necessarily ruins the self-respect of public employees, destroys the
> function of party in a republic, prostitutes elections into a desperate
> strife for personal profit, and degrades the national character by lower-
> ing the moral tone and standard of the country.

The object of civil service reform was to promote efficiency and honesty in the public service and to bring about the ethical regeneration of public life. Over bitter opposition from politicians, the reformers in 1883 passed the Pendleton Act, establishing a bipartisan Civil Service Commission, competitive examinations, and appointment on merit. The Pendleton Act also gave the president authority to extend by executive order the number of "classified" jobs—that is, jobs subject to the merit system. The act applied initially only to about 14,000 of the more than 100,000 federal positions. But by the end of the 19th century 40 percent of federal jobs had moved into the classified category.

Civil service reform was in part a response to the growing complexity of American life. As society grew more organized and problems more technical, official duties were no longer so plain and simple that any person of intelligence could perform them. In public service, as in other areas, the all-round man was yielding ground to the expert, the amateur to the professional. The excesses of the spoils system thus provoked the counter-ideal of scientific public administration, separate from politics and, as far as possible, insulated against it.

The cult of the expert, however, had its own excesses. The idea that administration could be divorced from policy was an illusion. And in the realm of policy, the expert, however much segregated from partisan politics, can never attain perfect objectivity. He remains the prisoner of his own set of values. It is these values rather than technical expertise that determine fundamental judgments of public policy. To turn over such judgments to experts, moreover, would be to abandon democracy itself; for in a democracy final decisions must be made by the people and their elected representatives. "The business of the expert," the British political scientist Harold Laski rightly said, "is to be on tap and not on top."

Politics, however, were deeply ingrained in American folkways. This meant intermittent tension between the presidential government, elected every four years by the people, and the permanent government, which saw presidents come and go while it went on forever. Sometimes the permanent government knew better than its political masters; sometimes it opposed or sabotaged valuable new initiatives. In the end a strong president with effective cabinet secretaries could make the permanent government responsive to presidential purpose, but it was often an exasperating struggle.

The struggle within the executive branch was less important, however, than the growing impatience with bureaucracy in society as a whole. The 20th century saw a considerable expansion of the federal establishment. The Great Depression and the New Deal led the national government to take on a variety of new responsibilities. The New Deal extended the federal regulatory apparatus. By 1940, in a nation of 130 million people, the number of federal workers for the first time passed the 1 million mark. The Second World War brought federal civilian employment to 3.8 million in 1945. With peace, the federal establishment declined to around 2 million by 1950. Then growth resumed, reaching 2.8 million by the 1980s.

The New Deal years saw rising criticism of "big government" and "bureaucracy." Businessmen resented federal regulation. Conservatives worried about the impact of paternalistic government on individual self-reliance, on community responsibility, and on economic and personal freedom. The nation in effect renewed the old debate between Hamilton and Jefferson in the early republic, although with an ironic exchange of positions. For the Hamiltonian constituency, the "rich and well-born," once the advocate of affirmative government, now condemned government intervention, while the Jeffersonian constituency, the plain people, once the advocate of a weak central government and of states' rights, now favored government intervention.

In the 1980s, with the presidency of Ronald Reagan, the debate has burst out with unusual intensity. According to conservatives, government intervention abridges liberty, stifles enterprise, and is inefficient, wasteful, and arbitrary. It disturbs the harmony of the self-adjusting market and creates worse troubles than it solves. Get government off our backs, according to the popular cliché, and our problems will solve themselves. When government is necessary, let it be at the local level, close to the people. Above all, stop the inexorable growth of the federal government.

In fact, for all the talk about the "swollen" and "bloated" bureaucracy, the federal establishment has not been growing as inexorably as many Americans seem to believe. In 1949, it consisted of 2.1 million people. Thirty years later, while the country had grown by 70 million, the federal force had grown only by 750,000. Federal workers were a smaller percentage of the population in 1985 than they were in 1955—or in 1940. The federal establishment, in short, has not kept pace with population growth. Moreover, national defense and the postal service account for 60 percent of federal employment.

Why then the widespread idea about the remorseless growth of government? It is partly because in the 1960s the national government assumed new and intrusive functions: affirmative action in civil rights, environmental protection, safety and health in the workplace, community organization, legal aid to the poor. Although this enlargement of the federal regulatory role was accompanied by marked growth in the size of government on all levels, the expansion has taken place primarily in state and local government. Whereas the federal force increased by only 27 percent in the 30 years after 1950, the state and local government force increased by an astonishing 212 percent.

Despite the statistics, the conviction flourishes in some minds that the national government is a steadily growing behemoth swallowing up the liberties of the people. The foes of Washington prefer local government, feeling it is closer to the people and therefore allegedly more responsive to popular needs. Obviously there is a great deal to be said for settling local questions locally. But local government is characteristically the government of the locally powerful. Historically, the way the locally powerless have won their human and constitutional rights has often been through appeal to the national government. The national government has vindicated racial justice against local bigotry, defended the Bill of Rights against local vigilantism, and protected natural resources against local greed. It has civilized industry and secured the rights of labor organizations. Had the states' rights creed prevailed, there would perhaps still be slavery in the United States.

The national authority, far from diminishing the individual, has given most Americans more personal dignity and liberty than ever before. The individual freedoms destroyed by the increase in national authority have been in the main the freedom to deny black Americans their rights as citizens; the freedom to put small children to work in mills and immigrants in sweatshops; the freedom to pay starvation wages, require barbarous working hours, and permit squalid working conditions; the freedom to deceive in the sale of goods and securities; the freedom to pollute the environment—all freedoms that, one supposes, a civilized nation can readily do without.

"Statements are made," said President John F. Kennedy in 1963, "labelling the Federal Government an outsider, an intruder, an adversary. . . . The United States Government is not a stranger or not an enemy. It is the people of fifty states joining in a national effort. . . . Only a great national effort by a great people working together can explore the mysteries of space, harvest the products at the bottom of the ocean, and mobilize the human, natural, and material resources of our lands."

So an old debate continues. However, Americans are of two minds. When pollsters ask large, spacious questions—Do you think government has become too involved in your lives? Do you think government should stop regulating business?—a sizable majority opposes big government. But when asked specific questions about the practical work of government—Do you favor social security? unemployment compensation? Medicare? health and safety standards in factories? environmental protection? government guarantee of jobs for everyone seeking employment? price and wage controls when inflation threatens?—a sizable majority approves of intervention.

In general, Americans do not want less government. What they want is more efficient government. They want government to do a better job. For a time in the 1970s, with Vietnam and Watergate, Americans lost confidence in the national government. In 1964, more than three-quarters of those polled had thought the national government could be trusted to do right most of the time. By 1980 only one-quarter was prepared to offer such trust. But by 1984 trust in the federal government to manage national affairs had climbed back to 45 percent.

Bureaucracy is a term of abuse. But it is impossible to run any large organization, whether public or private, without a bureaucracy's division of labor and hierarchy of authority. And we live in a world of large organizations. Without bureaucracy modern society would collapse. The problem is not to abolish bureaucracy, but to make it flexible, efficient, and capable of innovation.

Two hundred years after the drafting of the Constitution, Americans still regard government with a mixture of reliance and mistrust—a good combination. Mistrust is the best way to keep government reliable. Informed criticism is the means of correcting governmental inefficiency, incompetence, and arbitrariness; that is, of best enabling government to play its essential role. For without government, we cannot attain the goals of the Founding Fathers. Without an understanding of government, we cannot have the informed criticism that makes government do the job right. It is the duty of every American citizen to know our government—which is what this series is all about.

An air traffic controller monitors flight patterns on a radar screen. The FAA directs the air traffic control system to safeguard the nation's airways.

ONE

Controlling the Airways

The Federal Aviation Administration (FAA) is an agency of the U.S. government that has existed in various forms and under somewhat different names since 1926, when Congress passed the first of many federal aviation laws, the Air Commerce Act. Almost all of the FAA's work has to do with air safety: It licenses pilots and other flight personnel; it issues airworthiness certificates to new airplanes; it operates a nationwide air traffic control system; it manages a program to improve airports—all of which are locally owned—through the payment of federal subsidy money; and from time to time it has been involved in such activities as developing a transport plane that can fly faster than the speed of sound.

In 1926 very few persons had flown in an airplane; today more than half the adult population of the United States has made at least one commercial airplane flight. Then, commercial aviation was a struggling infant among U.S. businesses; today the commercial airlines constitute one of the major industries in America.

In 1926 after long debate, Congress decided that the authorities of the Department of Commerce who were responsible for air safety could impose civil penalties—fines, for example, for violation of air safety regulations. This

15

On December 17, 1903, at Kitty Hawk, North Carolina, Orville and Wilbur Wright became the first men to successfully fly a powered heavier-than-air machine. The flight, with Orville as pilot, covered a distance of 120 feet and lasted approximately 12 seconds.

law formed the foundation upon which the FAA would be built, but as aviation grew, the problems of air safety multiplied, and increased government activity was needed to deal with them. Today, the Federal Aviation Administration is more than a hundred times larger than the original Air Commerce Branch of the Department of Commerce.

The dramatic growth of commercial aviation could not have occurred, however, without the groundwork of the FAA. Under the FAA's guidance, the primitive airway system established as a result of the Air Commerce Act—a system that relied on lighted beacons and bonfires to guide pilots in bad weather and at night—was gradually replaced with a highly complex system of electronic beams that provide precise guidance signals to all airplanes equipped with suitable radios. Airports, still the responsibility of cities and local authorities, are periodically modernized with the aid of a multi-billion-dollar federal aid fund that is financed by a tax on airline tickets and air cargo waybills.

Claude Graham White attracts a crowd of spectators as he flies over Pennsylvania Avenue in Washington, D.C., in 1910. Prior to World War I, most private flying was done by a few wealthy men and women who were unlicensed and who flew planes that were not inspected for safety.

17

Given these major responsibilities, it is hard to imagine commercial aviation *without* the FAA, but in fact there were many both in and out of government in the 1920s who saw no need for government supervision of airlines. But that would soon change. In the early days of flying in the United States, the army dominated the skies. It bought one of the first planes built by the brothers Orville and Wilbur Wright, who, in 1903 at Kitty Hawk, North Carolina, were the first men to successfully fly a powered heavier-than-air machine. Private flying before the First World War was limited to a few wealthy men and women who bought Wright Flyers or small two-seaters from the other successful plane builder of the time, Glenn Curtiss. (Curtiss, an engine-builder and motorcycle racer from Hammondsport, New York, began to study and experiment with heavier-than-air machines in 1904, flew the first successful seaplane in 1911, and built the first flying boat in 1912. His factories turned out thousands of airplanes for the Allies during World War I.) The Post Office Department took on the only commercial flying activity and had early recognized the value of flying the mail, as opposed to carrying it by train or truck.

When World War I ended in 1918 the army was saddled with a large number of surplus warplanes that it did not want. It gave a boost to both private and commercial flying by making these unwanted planes available to the public at very low prices. The army also discharged a large number of pilots who had learned to fly at the taxpayers' expense. Many of these fliers bought the army's surplus planes and looked for ways to earn a living with them.

It was this fleet of surplus warplanes, flown by pilots who had learned to fly in World War I, that constituted civil aviation in America during the early 1920s. The surplus warplanes were used in many ingenious ways—from giving sight-seeing flights to the curious and the more daring spectators at air shows to photographing the nation's terrain for mapmaking. Regularly scheduled passenger flights along established intercity routes, so common today, were unknown at the time.

One reason that scheduled commercial aviation was slow in getting started in the United States was air safety—or the lack of it. Aircraft were unlicensed and uninspected. Anyone could proclaim himself or herself a pilot after completing the briefest instruction in takeoffs and landings. Aviation weather forecasting was in its infancy. Airfields were few and far between; when a pilot did arrive at an airfield it was usually unmarked, except for wheel ruts. Often the airfield was little more than a few flat acres of a local farmer's pastureland with a sign reading AIRPORT stuck on a post!

Without licensing, safety depended on the individual pilot and the airworthiness of the plane he or she flew. The airmail service, however, was an

18

An airfield in Chicago, Illinois, in 1928. Post–World War I airports were primitive by today's standards. There were no paved runways, few lighted beacons to guide pilots in bad weather or at night, and the planes were small and could not carry enough passengers to be profitable.

exception to this rule. As early as 1918 the U.S. Post Office Department had begun carrying the mail by air on its New York–Philadelphia–Washington route. By 1925 mail was being regularly moved over air routes established by the Post Office Department, using war-surplus planes owned by the Post Office and flown by carefully selected pilots who were employees of the federal government. Despite the airmail service's faster delivery time—mail could be flown from San Francisco to New York in approximately 33 hours, far less than the 72 hours required to carry it by train—the Post Office found it impossible to interest private businessmen in investing their money in aviation.

The contrast between the airmail service, with its experienced pilots who flew carefully maintained aircraft over established routes between well-marked airports, and the accident-prone civil fliers was evident to lawmakers as well as to the business community. But more was needed in addition to federal air-safety regulation. If Congress provided money for the development of national highways and seaways, why could it not fund the national airways as well?

In 1925 Congress responded to the call to encourage air service by passing the Kelly Airmail Act, which authorized the Post Office Department to contract with private operators to carry the mail. In 1926 Congress passed the Air Commerce Act, giving the Department of Commerce responsibility for air safety and providing for the establishment, operation, and maintenance of air routes. Provisions of both acts reassured businessmen that aviation could be a worthwhile investment.

The post–World War I generation of airplanes built by U.S. manufacturers was an important boost to the development of civil aviation in America. Although the first models were small by comparison with the giant jets in use today, they were a major leap forward. Both the Boeing Airplane Company and the Douglas Aircraft Company worked hard to produce planes that could carry enough passengers to be commercially profitable.

By 1936 the famous DC-3 twin-engine transport was being built by Douglas. It could seat 21 passengers and fly at about 273 km/h (170 mph), and therefore was profitable for its operators. However, it weighed 24,000 pounds and required a paved runway (at least during wet weather) for takeoffs and landings. But by 1938 only 231 airports out of a total of nearly 2,000 in the United States had paved runways, and of these only 36 had runways long enough to accommodate the DC-3. Much money was needed for airport improvements, and most of it would have to come from the federal Treasury.

When Congress passed the Civil Aeronautics Act in 1938 to clarify governmental authority and to set up a regulatory framework for the airlines and their investors, it was not principally in response to public pressure. As the FAA notes in its official history of the agency, "Air travel was still almost exclusively the province of the rich, and had little impact on the lives of the mass of Americans." In fact, the most important benefits from the Civil Aeronautics Act accrued to the airline industry. Prior to the act's passage, the airlines had to look to three different agencies for governmental regulation: the Post Office Department, which awarded all airmail contracts; the Interstate Commerce Commission, which established airmail rates; and the Bureau of Air

The first commercially successful aircraft, the Douglas DC-3, went into service in 1935. Designed to carry 21 passengers, it featured such advances as an all-metal stressed-skin construction, a radial engine, and retractable landing gear. By 1936 the Douglas DC-3 accounted for 95 percent of all U.S. commercial air traffic.

Commerce, which created and enforced regulations for aircraft operations and personnel.

The Civil Aeronautics Act, signed into law in 1938 by President Franklin D. Roosevelt, removed control of aviation from the Department of Commerce to a new and independent agency, the Civil Aeronautics Authority (CAA), which took over all of the duties previously carried out by the Post Office and Commerce departments. The CAA protected the established air carriers by stipulating that only those lines to which it had issued certificates would be allowed to operate scheduled air services and that operators could not establish new routes or discontinue existing ones without CAA approval.

In 1944 General Dwight D. Eisenhower, who was a licensed pilot, tries out the controls of a Martin B-26 bomber. In 1958, as president, Eisenhower signed legislation establishing the independent Federal Aviation Agency.

In 1940 President Roosevelt reorganized the CAA and created the Civil Aeronautics Board (CAB) to perform regulatory duties and accident investigations. The CAA was transferred back to the Commerce Department and remained there until 1958, when Congress created an independent organization called the Federal Aviation Agency (FAA) to supersede the CAA. The CAA was reorganized in an effort to cope with the doubling of aircraft speeds that followed the development of the jet transport plane in the 1950s and with the revolutionary influence of the jet on air travel. The creation of the new agency was the proposal of a planning group established by President Dwight D. Eisenhower, the first U.S. president to hold a private pilot's license.

Under the leadership of the 3 men who headed the independent FAA—U.S. Air Force generals Elwood R. Quesada (1959–60) and William F. McKee (1965–69) and the colorful lawyer and test pilot Najeeb E. Halaby (1961–65)—the FAA quickly developed into the eighth-largest agency in the federal government, with more than 43,000 employees and an annual budget of nearly three-quarters of a billion dollars.

The three independent administrators—independent in the sense that they reported directly to the president and were not part of any cabinet agency—set the pattern for the FAA as it exists today. In 1967 the FAA was placed under the newly created Department of Transportation (DOT). The responsibility for accident investigations was transferred from the CAB to the DOT's new autonomous National Transportation Safety Board, but the CAB remained an independent agency for commercial aviation until it was abolished in 1985. The FAA, whose administrator reports to the secretary of transportation, retains almost all its former responsibilities: air traffic control, both at airports and along the high- and low-altitude air routes that crisscross the nation; aid to airports and constant improvement of airway systems; licensing of pilots and other air personnel, including aircraft mechanics; research and testing of navigation aids, as well as investigation of medical problems associated with flight; and increasing involvement in the nationwide effort to catch drug smugglers and drug dealers.

Charles A. Lindbergh stands next to his plane The Spirit of St. Louis *on August 5, 1927—just two months after his historic solo nonstop flight from New York to Paris. Earlier in the decade, Lindbergh had earned money by wing-walking and barnstorming.*

TWO

Developing a New Resource

Air safety is the fundamental responsibility of the FAA. An important part of its effort is to prevent mid-air collisions, but even if there were only one airplane flying in the whole world, it could still crash. In fact, this is just what happened on a cool fall day in 1908.

Orville Wright was demonstrating the Wright Flyer to the Army Signal Corps at Fort Myer, Virginia (across the Potomac River from the nation's capital), when the plane went out of control and crashed. Orville suffered a broken leg and back injuries, and his passenger, Lieutenant Thomas Selfridge, was killed.

Today, an army accident board would investigate such a crash and issue a report on the cause of the accident. The FAA would take part in the accident investigation because a civilian pilot had been involved. At the time, however, Orville and his brother Wilbur were on their own; after the accident occurred they tried to reconstruct the final minutes of the flight in an effort to figure out what had gone wrong. They finally concluded that a mechanical failure involving the propeller had caused the crash. The Wright Flyer was later purchased by the War Department for the Army Signal Corps, despite Orville's accident at Fort Myer.

25

On September 9, 1908, Orville Wright demonstrates the Wright Flyer to the army at Fort Myer, Virginia. While Orville demonstrated the machine in the United States, Wilbur flew another plane in France, seeking the interest of a French manufacturer.

Military Aviation

Military aviation began even before the Wright brothers sold their Flyer to the Army Signal Corps. Observation balloons were used in the Civil War to spy on enemy defenses. The first military use of airplanes is credited to Italy, which

26

used planes on a small scale for reconnaissance and bombing in North Africa during the Italo-Turkish War of 1911–12. During World War I (1914–18), aviation rapidly expanded when the military potential of airplanes was recognized, first for observing battlefields and artillery fire, then for bombing land targets and air-to-air combat, called dogfighting. Special aircraft were designed to carry machine guns and bombs. Germany had relied on its zeppelins— cigar-shaped airships that could be steered—to launch night attacks on London and Paris; however, around 1914, after the advent of the airplane in combat, the zeppelins were easily intercepted. During the war, air squadrons of both sides played a secondary role to the land forces but were notable for their efforts in patrolling coastal areas and shipping lanes and in scouting for submarines. Planes were being designed to take off from ships, although carrier-based planes were not actually put into action during the war. By the

The first airplane passenger fatality—Lieutenant Thomas Selfridge— is carried away from the wreck of Orville Wright's plane. The accident occurred during a demonstration at Fort Myer on September 17, 1908.

Union soldiers hold the lines of an observation balloon, the Intrepid, *during the Civil War. Balloons were used by the military to direct artillery fire and to spy on enemy defenses.*

An army photographer takes pictures while on a reconnaissance mission in World War I. At the time, the army was not alone in using aerial photography; civilian pilots often flew photographers in their planes for mapmaking and surveying purposes.

war's end, dramatic improvements had been made in airplane design—resulting in greater speed, climbing ability, maneuverability, and load-bearing capacity.

After the Great War

After the war, the army offered the Curtiss JN-4H trainer, affectionately called a "Jenny," complete with engine for $300. (By comparison, a Curtiss OX-5 engine alone sold for $300.) It was a bargain, but what could a discharged pilot

A Curtiss JN-4H trainer, called a "Jenny," produced during World War I. The Jenny, which could be bought for $300 after the war, was the airplane most often used by barnstormers.

do with his own plane? The opportunities were limited. He—there were only a few women pilots—could earn a little money decorating his plane with advertising, even political advertising. He could put on shows for crowds at county and state fairs, with the aid of "wing walkers" who performed gymnastics on the outside of airplanes (they wore safety belts to keep from being blown off). He could even perform in movies, such as *Sky Highwayman* and *Speed Girl.* In 1928 *Wings* won the first Oscar ever given by the Motion Picture Academy for best picture of the year.

Aerial photography was in its infancy, but there was money to be made flying photographers high up enough so they could take pictures of entire cities. In 1920 one newspaper said that all of New York City was photographed in a little less than an hour. Crop dusting was another way the early fliers made money—Delta Airlines was started as a crop-dusting business in Louisiana in the early 1920s.

But the most popular way to earn money with an airplane was barnstorming. Offering "the thrill of the century," early pilots gave sightseeing rides to the curious, who would gather at a farmer's cow pasture to see the flying machine and its daring pilot. They were attracted to the impromptu airfield by the pilot himself, who often performed a few stunts over the nearest town before landing.

The farmer was paid for the use of his field with rides for himself and his family. Customers were charged whatever the traffic would bear, and the charges were raised or lowered depending on whether the stunt flying attracted a large crowd or a small one. A $5 bill for 10 minutes of sightseeing was considered a generous price for the barnstormer. When business dropped off, he flew away to greener pastures.

Because the rewards were so meager and the risks high—barnstormers had to contend with dangerous landing fields and constant breakdowns of engines and other vital parts of the airplane—only the most dedicated or the most foolhardy took up barnstorming as a way of life. Many pilots, such as Charles Lindbergh, wing-walked as a way to pay for flying lessons and then took up

A barnstormer flies upside down in an air show in 1924. After World War I, many pilots tried to make a living by daredevil flying and by offering sight-seeing rides.

barnstorming to get experience. Many others joined the Army Air Corps during the 1920s for the flying opportunities it offered.

Spare parts for old planes were hard to get, and many times a bit of baling wire, borrowed from the host farmer, was used to make repairs. In order to survive, a barnstormer had to be a skilled pilot, a good mechanic, a circus barker, and a shrewd business manager. One old barnstormer, when asked what the most dangerous part of his work was, answered: "the risk of starving to death." To escape this fate, not a few barnstormers took up "rum running"—smuggling whiskey into the United States during Prohibition (1919–33), when possession of alcoholic beverages was against the law.

Although these were the romantic days of early flight, there were also some serious efforts made to use airplanes for commercial purposes. One of the most successful of these was the airmail service. Carrying mail by plane had started as early as 1911 when, at a week-long air meet on Long Island, mail was collected in Garden City and flown a few miles to the post office in Mineola.

In 1918 Congress appropriated $100,000 to establish an experimental airmail route. Washington–New York was picked by the Post Office Department, and the army was asked to provide pilots and planes. The service began well, but when the novelty had worn off, so did the number of letters and cards being posted by airmail. The problem—and it still exists—was that the two cities are located so close together that the time saved by flying the mail was not significant. The experiment was an operational success, however. Almost all of the flights were operated on time; when weather caused cancellations, the mail was moved by train or truck.

The Post Office Department was sufficiently encouraged by its venture to open a transcontinental route in 1919. A few months after the start of the Cleveland-Chicago segment, New York was linked with Cleveland. In 1920 the transcontinental route was extended from Chicago to Omaha and then from Omaha to San Francisco. The first transcontinental flight occurred on February 22, 1921. The pilots were employees of the Post Office, and the planes they flew were war-surplus De Havilland DH-4's, developed by the British as bombers but modified according to Post Office specifications. The DH-4 was available in quantity, because it was produced in large numbers for wartime use by the army, but most of the planes came off the assembly lines too late for war service.

Barnstormers, army flying veterans, and others who applied for the job of Post Office pilot found that they were required to have 500 hours of flight time and to pass a qualifying examination. After acceptance the airmail pilots were given periodic medical examinations (today these are required of all pilots), and

On May 15, 1918, army pilot Lieutenant George Boyle prepares for takeoff from Washington, D.C. Boyle's flight inaugurated the Post Office Department's airmail service on the Washington–New York route.

their planes were carefully inspected according to a 180-item checklist after each mail run. There were fewer than 100 planes used, and these were maintained by a staff of 353 mechanics. Nearly 8 million miles were flown by the airmail service between 1922 and 1925 with only 10 fatal accidents—the best record of any type of flying at the time.

The successful airmail experiment was intended not only to demonstrate that mail could be carried routinely by air—today all first-class mail moves by air if it has to go any distance—but also, in the words of a federal study group, to serve "in the more important capacity of an experimental laboratory for the development of civil aviation." Businessmen in the 1920s were still concerned about two problems: air safety and the lack of federal regulation of air commerce. Without federal controls each state could enact its own laws to regulate aviation, and many did, creating serious complications for businesses of national scope.

When the Senate Commerce Committee held hearings on one of the many bills that had been introduced to regulate the infant aviation industry, it was surprised to find that no witnesses could be found to testify against the idea of federal regulation. "Congress has been denounced unsparingly for passing legislation regulating and controlling business," the committee report said. "It is rather startling, to say the least, to have an industry . . . asking and urging legislation putting the business completely under Federal control." At the same time, the committee discovered that there was no strong grass-roots support for such aviation legislation.

One of those who believed in federal legislation was a Chicago lawyer and former army pilot named William P. MacCracken, Jr. MacCracken, who had resumed his law practice after being discharged from the army, was retained to represent a pilot who had bought a small airfield near Chicago. As soon as the pilot closed the deal, the local tax collector appeared and announced, "You are running an amusement park and you have got to have a license." As MacCracken later related, "A license cost $200 . . . and my client just did not have $200." To make matters worse, MacCracken's client was taken before the local justice of the peace and fined an additional $200 for operating without a license. MacCracken took the case on appeal to the Municipal Court of Chicago and won it, after making an impassioned argument that an airfield was not an amusement park but a vital part of the fledgling business of air commerce.

Vital it may have been, but profitable it was not. In 1925, despite all the flying that was going on, scheduled air-passenger and freight service was virtually nonexistent, and the few commercial airports that existed struggled for survival. One of the few serious attempts to establish a commercial air-passenger line had failed in 1924. Even the air taxi companies were failing. Whereas in 1924 more than 100 airports reported that they offered some kind of on-demand passenger service, one year later their number had dropped to 60—despite the fact that the late 1920s were boom years for the U.S. economy.

Congress Takes Action

Congress was not idle during this time. By 1925 it had made more than 26 investigations—most of them safety related—into both civil and military aviation. Many of these resulted in proposed legislation, but none was passed by Congress because it was generally agreed that without a central federal authority to regulate and promote civil aviation, little progress in the commercial development of U.S. aviation could be expected.

Orville Wright, by then a highly respected figure in aviation, added his voice to the proregulators in 1924. "I believe the examination and licensing of every

A passenger boards a Boeing mail plane in 1928. After passage of the Kelly Air Mail Act in 1925, the Post Office Department divested itself of carrying mail and contracted with private companies.

pilot who engages in the transportation of passengers or merchandise for pay should be required," he said. "I also believe that proper precautions must be taken to insure the safe condition of the planes so used." Another respected figure, Assistant Postmaster General Paul Henderson, who had successfully operated the U.S. Air Mail Service, said that no serious businessman was likely to invest any substantial amount of money in aviation until Congress passed laws regulating who might pilot a plane, where he or she might fly, and in what kind of aircraft.

Secretary of Commerce Herbert Hoover (later president of the United States) wrote to one influential congressman that aviation "is the only industry that favors having itself regulated by the Government."

Safety regulation was important and needed, but the aviation community also hoped for more from the federal government. After all, the government dredged harbors to help shipping, financed the construction of highways and canals, and subsidized the westward expansion of railroads with land grants. If the federal government did all this for competing forms of transport, why should it not also develop the airways?

"There is no question that the development of commercial aviation requires that these things be done just as surely as there could have been no extensive motor car development . . . except that the States and Federal Government provided good roads," said airplane builder Chance M. Vought. A group of military fliers and their friends in Congress wanted to use the move towards government control of civil aviation to establish a unified civil-military aviation department with military men in charge. President Calvin Coolidge and other civilian officials in the government strongly opposed this idea.

"Water transportation for commercial purposes is not under the Navy Department and I have never known of anyone who wanted to put it there," argued William MacCracken, who was by now in the thick of the battle for federal control of civil aviation. As a first step, Congress passed the Kelly Air Mail Act (named after its sponsor, Representative Clyde Kelly of Pennsylvania) in January 1925. This law authorized the Post Office Department to divest itself of the job of carrying airmail and to contract out this work to private companies. (Congress was to some degree influenced by the powerful railroad lobby, which increasingly complained about the unfair competition with the government in transporting the mail.)

Both Congress and the business community knew that this law was the first step toward federal air-safety regulation and the development of airways and airports with federal support. Events moved quickly in Washington after passage of the Kelly Act. To assert his control over these events, President Coolidge appointed a special board of inquiry headed by Dwight W. Morrow to investigate the dramatic public charges brought by the air service's General Billy Mitchell, accusing the army and navy of gross incompetence and treachery in their refusal to recognize the importance of air power to the country's defense. (Mitchell was an advocate of an independent air force and of unified control of air power and was later court-martialed for insubordination.) Morrow, an investment banker and later an ambassador to Mexico (and father-in-law of Charles Lindbergh), was instructed by the president to examine the state of aviation in the United States and to make recommendations for furthering its development. President Coolidge had close ties to Morrow, whom he had first known when they were classmates at Amherst College. The unspoken task he had given Morrow was to counter the

Colonel Billy Mitchell (standing) is court-martialed for insubordination on December 17, 1925. After World War I, Mitchell, former assistant chief of the Air Service, championed air power and its revolutionary use by the military—in sinking battleships, for example; however, the War Department was unwilling to change its fighting traditions and found Mitchell's proposals provoking. In 1945 Congress voted to award posthumously to Mitchell the Medal of Honor and to promote him to the rank of major general.

In 1930 in Wauchula, Florida, businessmen pose in front of the airplane that will transport the first cargo of strawberries ever shipped by air. After the passage of the Air Commerce Act of 1926, which provided for the regulation of airways and licensing of pilots and aircraft, businessmen and bankers began to invest in commercial aviation.

movement toward a unified civil-military aviation department and to take the headlines away from Congress, where the civil versus military control of aviation debate raged anew.

Thus it was no surprise when the president's Aircraft Board, unofficially called the Morrow Board, recommended that civil and military aviation be kept separate. A department of aeronautics that combined civil and military aviation was "contrary to the principles under which the country has attained its present moral and material power," the Morrow Board reported. Congress agreed, and both the House of Representatives and the Senate passed bills giving the secretary of commerce the responsibility to regulate and foster air commerce and to maintain airways and aids to air navigation.

The final bill passed by Congress authorized the secretary to impose penalties for air-safety violations, but only fines and license suspensions, not jail sentences. The federal government had always established and maintained lighthouses and channel markers as well as maintaining and dredging channels and harbors, so airways were to become a federal responsibility also. Airports, however, were said to be comparable to ship docks, which had always been the responsibility of local authorities. It was believed that airport development would be a costly proposition and that federal aid for this purpose would be quite expensive.

President Coolidge signed the Air Commerce Act into law on May 20, 1926. The new law authorized the appointment of assistant secretaries for air in the Navy, Army, and Commerce departments. Secretary Hoover picked William MacCracken to be the first assistant secretary of commerce for air. His job was to promote aviation by providing for the licensing of pilots, the inspection of airplanes for safety purposes, and the establishment of airways to guide pilots. He was helped in his promotion efforts by Charles Lindbergh, whose nonstop flight across the Atlantic Ocean from New York to Paris in 1927 had made him a national hero.

MacCracken had appealed to Lindbergh for his help in encouraging aviation. Lindbergh obliged by flying congressmen on sight-seeing trips around Washington and by making a series of goodwill flights around the United States, attracting attention wherever he landed. Lindbergh was employed by Pan American World Airways to help expand its routes by flying exploratory missions to check air routes and landing fields. Later he also helped Trans World Airlines by allowing TWA to call itself the "Lindbergh Line." Another hero, Eddie Rickenbacker—the most celebrated U.S. pilot of World War I—was also active making speeches and personal appearances to promote commercial aviation, finally becoming president of Eastern Air Lines in 1938.

The Commerce Department's Bureau of Lighthouses took over the operation of airway beacons in 1927. When, in the same year, the Post Office Department contracted with the Boeing Airplane Company to fly the mail between San Francisco and Chicago, the Commerce Department also assumed responsibility for the air routes. The transfer from the Post Office Department to the Commerce Department involved 17 communication stations, 95 emergency landing fields, and other facilities, along with 146 former U.S. Air Mail Service employees.

The first airways developed by the Commerce Department followed the airmail routes. By mid-1927, the Aeronautics Branch was operating 2,080 miles of airways, including routes between New York and Boston, Chicago and

American ace Eddie Rickenbacker, photographed in his Spad fighter in France during World War I, actively promoted commercial aviation in the late 1920s by giving speeches and making personal appearances.

St. Louis, and Chicago and Dallas. When beacons were placed along the 2,041 miles of the transcontinental route, expansion rapidly followed. By 1933 the federal airway system was made up of 18,000 miles of lighted airways: 1,550 rotating beacons were in operation along with 263 emergency landing fields. Although the Commerce Department was short of the goal of 25,000 miles of lighted airways set by Assistant Secretary MacCracken, President Hoover was to say later that "I felt a personal triumph with every mile of service we added."

The 17 communication stations that were transferred from the Post Office to the Aeronautics Branch of the Commerce Department were basically telegraph stations. No voice communications existed, nor did any radio navigation beacons. Pilots could not communicate with each other or with ground stations. An air-to-ground communication system was considered an important safety need. With the help of the National Bureau of Standards (an agency of the Department of Commerce that provides measurement standards and practices for the United States), such a system was finally developed by 1928.

Considerable progress was made by the Aeronautics Branch when Franklin D. Roosevelt became president in 1932. But in the opening days of his administration economy in government was the watchword, and the Aeronautics Branch was cut back. As a result, air safety suffered.

When an air crash in 1935 caused the death of Bronson M. Cutting, a

Senator Bronson M. Cutting of New Mexico was killed in an airplane accident in 1935. Cutting's death prompted a congressional investigation of air safety that resulted in the appropriation of more money for improvements and the takeover by the government of the air traffic control centers in Newark, Chicago, and Cleveland.

well-liked U.S. senator from New Mexico, Congress responded with demands for improvements. The accident involving Senator Cutting had occurred during bad weather; the pilot had erred in continuing a flight he should have aborted, and the weather report had been misleading. Congress became belligerent over the death of one of its own and ordered an investigation. One immediate outcome of the investigation was the appropriation of more money for air safety; another was the takeover by the federal government of three of the most important air traffic control centers in the country: Newark, Chicago, and Cleveland.

A steward serves a meal to passengers aboard a transcontinental flight in the late 1930s. When it passed the Civil Aeronautics Act of 1938, Congress helped steady the airline industry by creating the Civil Aeronautics Authority to regulate airlines and the Air Safety Board to investigate airplane accidents.

The Civil Aeronautics Act of 1938

In 1938 Congress enacted new air safety legislation in the form of the Civil Aeronautics Act. It was a complicated law: In one piece of legislation Congress attempted to establish economic control over the aviation industry for the first time while continuing regulatory control over air safety. The act removed control of aviation from the Department of Commerce to a new and independent agency, the Civil Aeronautics Authority (CAA). The authority was run by a five-person commission, a three-person Air Safety Board, and an administrator. The authority's duties were distributed on a functional basis: The commission oversaw the legislative and judicial aspects of economic and safety regulation; the Air Safety Board investigated aviation accidents; and the administrator promoted civil aeronautics and air commerce in the United States and abroad and encouraged the creation and maintenance of airways, landing fields, and navigation facilities, and the development of aircraft. (Although the law had to be amended several times and completely rewritten on one occasion, the separation of accident investigation responsibility from regulatory duties continues today.)

The Pan American World Airways flying boat, capable of carrying 48 passengers, began regular service across the Pacific in 1935—making stops in Hawaii, Guam, and the Philippines. Pan Am did not begin its transatlantic flights from Long Island to England until 1939.

THREE

Building an Agency: From the CAA to the FAA

When the Civil Aeronautics Act was passed in 1938 nearly 3,000 employees were shifted to the CAA's payroll, making the Civil Aeronautics Authority one of the largest agencies in the government at the time. The new agency's size and the amount of money it spent (Congress appropriated more than $14 million to the CAA) attracted public and political attention, and the administrators of the CAA were criticized for ineffective management. After its first two years of operation, neither President Franklin D. Roosevelt nor Congress was pleased with the way the CAA was being run.

In 1940 President Roosevelt ordered the Bureau of the Budget to study the CAA and come up with a reorganization plan that would consolidate the three basic federal air-safety functions: safety recommendations and the determination of "probable cause" of air accidents; licensing of pilots, air personnel, and airplanes; and the economic regulation of the rapidly expanding commercial airlines, including the awarding of routes and the approval of fares. The reorganization plan recommended by the Bureau of the Budget proved difficult to get through Congress, but in the end President Roosevelt's plan prevailed—he issued two executive orders restructuring the agency. The first order

45

shifted all safety regulation (except for the writing of rules) from the five-person commission to the administrator. The administrator's agency was called the Civil Aeronautics Administration (CAA). The second order reaffirmed the authority of the Civil Aeronautics Board (CAB) and made the CAA and the CAB a part of the Department of Commerce once again. The Air Safety Board was disbanded and its functions were transferred to the CAB. However, the CAB was to retain the functions of rule making, of hearing and settling legal cases, and of investigating air safety and was to perform these duties independently, without any control by the secretary of commerce. This division of aviation responsibilities endured until well after the end of World War II.

The Inauguration of Transatlantic Service

Transatlantic service was started late in the 1930s by both the British Overseas Airways Company (BOAC) and by Pan American World Airways, using giant flying boats (seaplanes with a hull adapted for floating) built by such manufacturers as the Martin Company of Baltimore, Maryland, and Boeing Airplane Company of Seattle, Washington. (Boeing built the flying boat *Yankee Clipper*—the Pan American plane that made the first U.S. commercial transatlantic air trips from the channel at Port Washington, Long Island, to Southampton, England.)

At the start of World War II, with German submarines making travel by ship particularly hazardous, the transatlantic flying service of BOAC and Pan American became the principal link between the Americas and Europe, utilizing the neutrality of Portugal and the ability of Lisbon's harbor to accommodate the flying boats. In the United States, regulation of aviation tightened as the war clouds gathered.

On December 13, 1941, six days after the bombing of Pearl Harbor by the Japanese, President Roosevelt directed the secretary of commerce to "exercise control and jurisdiction over civil aviation in accordance with requirements for the successful prosecution of the war, as may be requested by the Secretary of War." An executive order signed by the president directed the secretary of war "to take possession of any civil aviation system or systems or any part thereof to the extent necessary to the successful prosecution of the war." One of the first steps taken under this directive was a request to the CAA to establish air-route traffic control centers, forming the basis for the system used today.

The CAA was also required to complete its planned nationwide traffic control communications network "in the interest of national defense." Even before the

Japanese bombers attack American navy planes at Pearl Harbor on December 7, 1941; on the following day, Congress declared war against Japan. One week after the attack on Pearl Harbor, President Franklin D. Roosevelt authorized the secretary of commerce, at the request of the secretary of war, to take over any civil aviation system necessary to help in combating enemy forces.

47

Top: *In 1943 U.S. Weather Bureau staff enters weather observation data from all areas of the country onto charts at Washington National Airport.* Bottom: *Pilots then receive the latest weather information from the Civil Aeronautics Administration's flight communications service—via radio.*

attack on Pearl Harbor, the CAA had taken actions to put the nation's air transport system on a war footing. At the request of the War Department, a number of airports were designated as essential to national defense, and the operation of their control towers was taken over by the CAA.

Shortly after the start of World War II the CAA, at the request of the War Department, worked with the Army Signal Corps to set up a worldwide network of navigation aids that could be used by the Air Transport Command, the military unit that provided air travel to military personnel. First priority was the flow of bombers and fighter aircraft being ferried to Britain. Navigation aids were set up along this transatlantic route, and construction was begun on a chain of navigation aids and airports in South America and Africa.

During the war the CAA continued to improve its services to both military and civilian pilots. One important improvement was in the area of communications. In 1943, for example, the CAA started up its flight communications service. This enabled pilots to use their radios to obtain the latest weather reports and forecasts along the routes they were flying. By the end of World War II, the CAA was a major factor in weather reporting and communications and had also expanded its network of navigation aids to include more than 200 locations outside the United States.

Also by the end of the war, the CAA was operating approximately 115 airport control towers, using both its own funds and those of the air force. Soon after the victory in Europe in 1945 the CAA ended its operation of control towers at 23 airports because of cuts in funding. The military continued to operate control towers at military airfields, and the CAA operated control towers at the major civilian fields. This division of responsibility worked reasonably well, even in locations such as Washington, D.C., where an air force field, a navy field, and a civilian airport were clustered close together.

Postwar Activities

During World War II, the United States had developed a number of efficient transport craft that would give it a head start in postwar commercial aviation. Britain, which had been compelled to abandon civil transport development in favor of the urgently needed military aircraft, now acted to prevent the U.S. airlines from dominating international civil air routes after the war ended. In November 1944, a conference was called in Chicago, Illinois, to draft an international agreement concerning civil aviation. Representatives of all members of the United Nations except the Soviet Union attended the meeting and established the International Civil Aviation Organization (ICAO), still in existence today, to ensure the safe development of aviation worldwide. The ICAO's duties are to encourage the creation of airways, airports and air navigation facilities, and the art of airplane design. It also endeavors to meet international needs for safe, efficient, and economical air travel and to do all it can to ensure that there is no unfair competition between contracting nations. The CAA, as the U.S. agency regulating civil aviation at the time, worked closely with the ICAO in administering the international policies.

In the year following the war, the regulatory and promotional efforts of civil aviation were steadily improving—airplane manufacturers were producing faster and bigger aircraft, mandatory flight recorders provided on-board monitoring of aircraft equipment, and radar was installed at selected airports. But other postwar activities created problems for the CAA: Airport locations and zoning requirements resulted in major disputes between the CAA and local

In 1956 Elwood Quesada, second from right, photographed here in the late 1920s, was named to a commission by President Dwight D. Eisenhower to study the effect of jets on air traffic control and to make recommendations for solving the congestion problem at airports.

officials. While it wrestled with the problems of noise pollution and the overbooking of flights, the CAA also had to balance concerns about flight safety with the airlines' demands for increased profits. By 1954, with the advent of jets, the CAA was having difficulty in regulating the aviation industry.

Everybody knew that the time had come to place all air traffic control under a single agency, but it took a disaster to stir Congress into action. On June 30, 1956, two planes collided in midair over northern Arizona, killing 128 people. The planes took off within three minutes of each other from Los Angeles International Airport. They were flying parallel courses (one was headed for Kansas City, Missouri, and the other for Chicago, Illinois) as they headed into heavy thunderstorms, collided, and then crashed less than one mile apart. Congressional hearings revealed air traffic control was a divided responsibility, that funds for the Civil Aeronautics Administration were inadequate—especially those for navigation aids and air traffic control facilities—and that air traffic controllers were woefully underpaid.

President Dwight D. Eisenhower named two wartime air force generals to help him look into the matter of setting up an independent federal aviation agency. General Elwood Quesada and General Edward P. Curtis (a World War I flier and later an official of the Eastman Kodak Company) were named to a commission to study the impact of jets on air traffic control and the means of dealing with increasing congestion at airports. After its investigation, the commission proposed the creation of a new federal aviation agency that would replace the CAA.

The Federal Aviation Agency

In 1958 Congress created an organization independent of the Commerce Department called the Federal Aviation Agency (FAA) to supersede the CAA, and General Quesada was named its first administrator. The CAB continued the economic regulation of air transportation and the investigation of accidents. The Federal Aviation Agency took over the CAB's responsibilities for establishing air-safety regulations and for revoking and suspending safety certificates.

Because the proposal for an independent federal aviation agency had been backed by two air force generals and had been supported by President Eisenhower (who had been a career military officer and supreme commander of the Allied forces in Europe during World War II), the military services were finally persuaded to accept the idea of civilian control over all air traffic in the

United States. To quiet the fears of military commanders that they would be excluded from the federal aviation agency's operation, it was agreed that the military would play an important role in the agency, and that in the event of a major war all air traffic controllers would automatically become part of the military services.

Another uproar for reorganization of the FAA occurred during the presidency of Lyndon Johnson when the American public demanded major transportation reform. Consumer groups pressured Congress to address transportation safety, especially safety standards in the automobile industry. President Johnson sent a proposal to Congress to create a federal transportation department that would tackle the safety concerns and would include such agencies as the U.S. Coast Guard, the Bureau of Public Roads, and the Federal Aviation Agency. He gained Congress's support of his plan, and in April 1967 the independent Federal Aviation Agency was renamed the Federal Aviation Administration (FAA) and transferred to the Department of Transportation (DOT). The CAB's responsibility for accident investigations was assigned to the newly created National Transportation Safety Board.

A New FAA Tackles the Job

Just as its forerunners did, the FAA has to contend with the problem of mixing military and civilian planes together on both high- and low-altitude air routes and at joint-use airports. When General Quesada headed the agency, the air force was accommodated in its demand that the military have a key role in its operation. Congress, in setting up the FAA, made this possible by specifying that although no FAA administrator could be a military officer on active duty, such an officer could serve as deputy administrator.

All this maneuvering was brought about by the growth of military aviation, not only in the air force but in the navy and the army as well. In the U.S. airspace, except for certain restricted areas specifically designated for military flying, the FAA has the job of controlling both military and civilian air traffic.

The Supersonic Transport Program

An important task—development of a commercial transport plane that could fly faster than the speed of sound—had been assigned by President Johnson to Administrator William McKee in 1965. That the FAA should lead the effort to

Major General William F. McKee in 1950. In 1965 McKee was appointed by President Lyndon B. Johnson to head the Federal Aviation Agency. One of his first tasks as administrator was to help develop a supersonic transport plane.

develop a new supersonic transport (SST) might at first seem surprising. Apart from the research and development of new navigation aids, the FAA does not ordinarily spend much of its time on new aircraft development. The National Aeronautics and Space Administration (NASA) usually handles research in the area of aircraft technology. But the FAA is charged with the promotion of aviation, and certainly a supersonic transport would promote air travel—that is, if one could be designed and built to operate economically.

The SST project was not entirely outside the FAA's line of work. In 1963, for example, the FAA held a design competition for a small modern transport that could be useful to both the local service carriers and the government. The competition ended the year after it started with the statement by FAA officials that "none of the designs submitted was considered to represent a sufficient advance in the state of the art to warrant award of a detailed design contract." Despite this comment, the effort was considered to be part of the FAA's job of promoting aviation.

During the SST program, even the fine management effort given by the FAA under the direction of Administrator McKee was not sufficient to produce a commercially useful plane. One difficulty that could not be overcome with the technology available in the 1960s was the excessive fuel consumption of such a high-speed aircraft. This, coupled with the severe shortage of oil, which in turn led to soaring prices for jet fuel, doomed the SST project. Public interest groups, such as Friends of the Earth and Sierra Club, protested the SST program and directed their attacks at the FAA for not considering the negative effects that the plane's sonic boom and air pollution would have on the environment.

The British and the French, with their supersonic Concorde planes, also ran into the high-cost fuel barrier. However, they were further along in their project than were the Americans and they grimly paid subsidy money, first to build approximately 20 Concordes and then to the airlines—British Airways and Air France—that bought and operated them.

After the FAA dropped out of the SST effort in 1971, interest was kept alive by NASA and by some of the private plane builders, such as Boeing and Lockheed. The FAA continues to be interested in supersonic flight, if for no

A full-scale mock-up of the Lockheed SST, or supersonic transport. The FAA became embroiled in the debate over whether the United States should build a commercial aircraft capable of flying at super- sonic speeds; finally, in 1971, its efforts to build the plane failed— largely because of economic, technological, and environmental issues raised by the American public.

54

In 1962 Great Britain and France signed an agreement to build an SST that could fly at twice the speed of sound. The result was the Concorde; one is shown here at Dulles International Airport in Washington, D.C.

other reason than its responsibility for issuing an airworthiness certificate to any U.S.-built SST that might be used to carry passengers commercially.

The Airline Deregulation Act of 1978

A major change in government procedure occurred on October 24, 1978, when the Airline Deregulation Act was adopted. The act provided for a decrease in airline regulation and an increase in competition. The CAB was instructed to be less restrictive in responding to carrier initiatives involving fares and the establishment of routes, and its regulatory functions were to be phased out by 1984, with the CAB itself to be abolished in 1985. Congress had believed that the carrier fares and performance of the intrastate (non-CAB regulated) airlines were preferable to those of the CAB-regulated airlines. They also

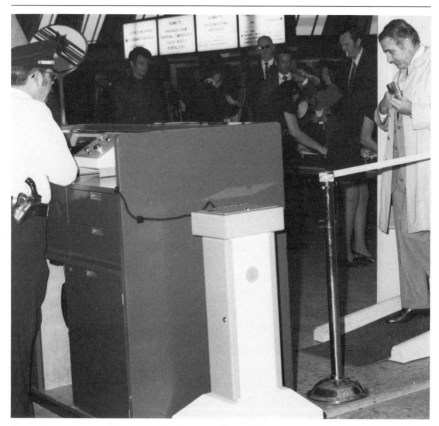

An airport security guard observes boarding passengers. In the 1980s the FAA tightened regulations for airport security after a rash of hijackings at foreign airports.

agreed that competition was to be encouraged as a way to increase efficiency, modernization, and lower prices. The provisions of the act applied to domestic air transportation; foreign transportation was largely unchanged by the act.

Since passage of the Airline Deregulation Act, the number of commercial airlines serving the United States has increased enormously. Air fares have generally fallen, and the airlines have been free to choose air routes that seem to be the most profitable, but deregulation has not been entirely beneficial to airports. Airlines, vying for the most popular routes, have overburdened air traffic control at major airports and have left many other airports without regular air service. The problems of noise and air pollution and the lack of terminal space have also been compounded at hub airports. (The hub idea

56

brings in passengers from outlying cities and redirects them outbound on the same carrier's planes. This requires a choreographed arrival and departure schedule in order to keep a passenger from transferring to another airline that offers a better schedule.)

Airport Security and the War on Drugs

Among the special projects that kept the FAA in the headlines after the SST program was abandoned were the problems of hijacking, terrorism, and dealing with pilots, particularly of small planes, who tried to smuggle drugs into the United States.

Policemen with submachine guns patrol the Leonardo da Vinci International Airport in Rome, Italy, in 1985 after a commando squad of Arab rebels attacked an office and killed 15 people, wounding more than 75 others. The FAA has the authority to ban U.S. planes from using foreign airports where lax security measures endanger U.S. air service.

A U.S. Customs Service plane (right) chases a drug smuggler. To help in the effort to fight the illegal import of narcotics and other drugs, the FAA has issued rules requiring pilots to give position reports and obtain clearances before entering U.S. border areas.

Airport security was lax in a number of places around the world, and although the FAA is required to license airports in the United States, its responsibilities are not that direct at foreign airports. Nevertheless, the FAA is concerned about the security procedures used at any airport where U.S. planes land and can ban these planes from using airports where security is so poor as to present a threat to U.S. air services.

The airport in Athens, Greece, attracted much of the FAA's attention in the early 1980s because it was the site frequently used by hijackers to board aircraft they had singled out for seizure. Pressure by U.S. authorities, including the FAA, caused the Greek government to actively improve security at the Athens airport, and the hijackers stayed away after the Greek government let it be known that they would do all they could to combat them.

Drug smuggling during most of the 1980s was often the work of small-plane owners and pilots who counted on being able to make one or two profitable runs undetected. Much of the smuggling occurred across the southern border of the United States, with flights originating in Mexico and Colombia and landing in Florida and Texas.

The FAA, in its effort to contribute to the war on drugs in the mid-1980s, issued a number of regulations intended to deter smugglers. One regulation required a special permit before long-range fuel tanks could be installed in an aircraft. Another stipulation required that pilots give position reports to the FAA and obtain clearances before entering the coastal areas of the United States. Violators risked no more than license suspension, because the FAA has never had the authority to jail anyone, even pilots who were obviously and flagrantly drunk.

Controllers on Strike

The air traffic controllers alone account for more than a third of the FAA staff. Even though air traffic has continued to increase steadily during the 1970s and 1980s, the number of controllers has actually decreased since 1981, when the FAA fired 12,000 members of the Professional Air Traffic Controllers Organization (PATCO) after they walked off their job in an illegal strike. The union demanded, among other things, a $10,000 pay increase for each controller, a shorter workweek, early retirement, and more respect from the supervisors. After rejecting Secretary of Transportation Drew Lewis's offer of a 34 percent pay increase over a period of three years, the controllers decided to strike in violation of federal law, believing that air transportation could not function without them. President Ronald Reagan ordered them to return to work within 48 hours. When the controllers refused, they were all fired.

After the dismissal of the 12,000 PATCO members, the FAA took extraordinary measures to keep the air traffic control system working. Military controllers were brought in from the armed forces, supervisors were pressed into service, and senior controllers were kept on the job past retirement age. All contributed to meet the challenge of continuing air traffic control.

The problems of air traffic control had been serious long before the PATCO strike in 1981. Ronald Reagan, during the course of his campaign for the presidency in 1980, had said, "I have been thoroughly briefed by members of my staff as to the deplorable state of the nation's air traffic control system. They have told me that too few people working unreasonable hours with

59

Striking air traffic controllers hold hands as they ignore the back-to-work deadline issued by President Ronald Reagan on August 5, 1981. The FAA fired more than 12,000 PATCO members when they refused to go back to work.

Transportation Secretary Drew Lewis (left) and FAA administrator Lynn Helms respond to reporters during a press conference in which they announced the firing of the striking air traffic controllers.

obsolete equipment have placed the nation's travelers in unwarranted danger."

Ironically, in 1988 at the end of Reagan's presidency, the same conclusion was being drawn by critics of the FAA who believed that the agency had been too slow in rebuilding the air traffic control system after the 1981 strike. The actual decision to fire the striking controllers was made by President Reagan's secretary of transportation, Drew Lewis. What made the situation worse for air travelers and airlines alike, however, was President Reagan's refusal to allow any of the fired controllers to return to work despite the need for their skills and the financial hardships they were enduring. Although Congress has repeatedly tried to lift the ban on rehiring the controllers who went on strike—a law to this effect was vetoed by President Reagan—the FAA has continued to put up with controller shortages since the strike. (In 1987, six years after the strike, those who had stayed on the job were joined by new employees in forming a new controllers union to deal with their still unresolved workplace problems.)

Another unfortunate consequence of the firing of the 12,000 air traffic controllers was that the FAA—lacking enough trained controllers to handle all the air traffic and to maintain a reasonable margin of safety, particularly at peak hours—had instituted a slowdown. Controllers simply held aircraft on the ground until the system could safely accommodate them. Many passengers boarded their planes only to be told that there would be delayed takeoff; in some cases the delays amounted to an hour or more, causing consternation among passengers who had to make connecting flights at their destination.

The passengers complained bitterly to the flight crews, who of course could do nothing about the delays—although one pilot taxied his plane back to the gate one day, announced to the passengers that he was taking immediate retirement from his job because he was "fed up" with the delays, and got off the plane, never to fly for an airline again. Some passengers were congressmen and airline officials, so the FAA had to put up with a constant barrage of criticism as a result of its air traffic control delays.

To solve these problems, the FAA has begun a massive upgrade of its systems—especially its air traffic control systems. It is planning for better radars, new computers, more reliable radio communication equipment, and improved navigation and weather-reporting capabilities such as the Doppler weather radars that can detect the dangerous wind-shear conditions at airports. (The Doppler radar system is based on the Doppler effect, a change in frequency of sound or light resulting from the motion of a source in relation to an observer. For example, when a storm moves toward an observer the sound waves it produces are closer together than they are when the storm moves away from the observer. The radar measures the speed of the waves.) Wind shear is an extreme shift in wind speed and direction that can abruptly stop the normal lift-producing flow of air over a plane's wings and that can lead to disaster. It is too often the cause of crashes that occur during takeoffs and landings.

The $12 billion, 10-year "national aerospace" program to upgrade the FAA's ability to deal with present and future air traffic growth had fallen behind schedule by the mid-1980s, and the agency was drawing sharp criticism from the aviation industry and Congress.

When Donald D. Engen, a retired Navy flier and former member of the National Transportation Safety Board, took over as administrator of the FAA in 1984, he ordered his staff to step up safety inspections of the airlines and of the smaller regional and air taxi companies as well. The two-year intensive inspection program was conducted by the FAA to bring the airlines into compliance with FAA safety regulations. Some of the inspections took as long as two months or more, and the FAA assigned from 7 to 32 specialists to each of the inspections. The FAA said its inspection teams "look at every aspect of an airline's operations and maintenance programs to see if they comply with federal regulations, FAA guidance materials, and company policies. Where

People stranded at New York's Kennedy Airport during the air traffic controllers' strike await news about their departing flights. The FAA brought in military controllers to help keep the system running during the imbroglio.

deficiencies are uncovered, the airline is required to develop a plan of corrective action which must be approved by the agency. Civil penalty actions may also be initiated if circumstances warrant."

The inspection program resulted in a spate of fines during the mid-1980s, and some small aviation companies were put out of business by the FAA. Widespread publicity was given to the heavy fines imposed on well-known airlines for safety violations. Eastern Airlines (taken over by Texas Air Corporation in 1986) drew the largest fine, $9.8 million, whereas Delta had to pay $140,000 for 11 violations. Most of the violations were record-keeping failures, some caused by nothing more than computer malfunctions, but there were some serious air safety violations uncovered as well.

Early in 1987 Administrator Engen told reporters that although there had been no fatal accidents in 1986 involving U.S. commercial airlines in scheduled passenger service, "One year does not a safety record make." In 1985 the accident record, particularly in overseas air transportation, was a poor one. With more planes being held on the ground for safety purposes, the FAA was successful in keeping the domestic accident rates down, but at the cost of increased delays for passengers. Taking note of the rising number of complaints about delays, Administrator Engen said that the fault was partly that of the

Donald D. Engen, a former member of the National Transportation Safety Board, was appointed FAA administrator in 1984. Engen immediately ordered his aviation safety staff to increase safety inspections of commercial airlines, including the smaller regional operators.

In 1987 Secretary of Transportation James Burnley IV (left) and FAA administrator T. Allan McArtor discuss the record-breaking fine—$9.8 million—imposed on Eastern Airlines for its safety violations.

airlines for over scheduling flights at crowded hub airports. To speed up the air traffic system, the FAA in 1987 expanded the number of air routes available in the northeastern portion of the United States. This move, along with increased recruitment of air traffic controllers and accelerated controller training, was successful in reducing some of the delays that were drawing so many complaints. So that the airlines could sit down together and work out solutions to their over-scheduling problems, the Department of Transportation was given the power to grant the airlines immunity from antitrust laws (laws that regulate or prohibit unfair business competition) because dividing up scarce time periods at overcrowded airports is a form of restraint of trade and would normally bring down the wrath of the Department of Justice on the airlines.

In the 1990s the FAA plans to reduce traffic delays at airports by altering routes. When new computers are installed by the FAA in the early 1990s air traffic controllers will be able to track down automatically the movement of each plane under control and to obtain the plane's identification number, speed, and altitude. The controllers will then be able to change the flight plans for all planes on a particular route, enabling them to avoid delays and bad weather merely by punching a new route into the computer. The controller will radio the new route to the plane's crew while the computer automatically updates the electronic displays that other controllers might need to refer to.

The airport traffic control tower at Van Nuys, California. The FAA has approximately 328 operating towers and more than 9,000 controllers working in them; the number of controllers in a tower varies from 10 to 150.

FOUR

The FAA Today

The Federal Aviation Administration is the largest agency in the Department of Transportation (DOT). Its administrator is the principal adviser to the secretary and deputy secretary of transportation on civil aviation and air transportation matters and directs the agency and its more than 48,000 employees from FAA headquarters at 800 Independence Avenue in southwest Washington, D.C. In 1988 the administrator managed a budget of more than $6 billion.

Over the years, the administrator has been nominated by the president, subject to confirmation by the Senate. Former military officers of high rank are a principal recruiting source for the office. In almost all cases, the administrator has been a pilot, usually a military pilot, the idea being that an agency dealing with pilots should preferably be directed by someone with firsthand experience. General William F. McKee, who served as FAA administrator from 1965 to 1969, was an exception to this rule. Although General McKee was an air force officer, his specialties were procurement (purchasing aircraft and related equipment) and managing complex programs involving the maintenance and transportation of material for the military.

In one way or another, every one of the functions performed by the FAA—and correspondingly by the administrator—is related to air safety. Among its numerous activities are: regulating air commerce to promote

67

development and safety and to meet the requirements of national defense; controlling the use of navigable U.S. airspace and regulating both civil and military operations in this airspace, in the interest of safety and efficiency; promoting, encouraging, and developing civil aeronautics; incorporating the results of research undertaken to improve air navigation facilities; installing and operating air navigation facilities; developing and operating a common system of air traffic control and navigation for both civil and military aircraft; and working out programs and establishing regulations to control aircraft noise, sonic boom, air pollution, and the other environmental effects of civil aviation.

FAA Management

The administrator is directly assisted by a deputy administrator, an associate administrator, four assistant administrators, and four executive directors. The deputy administrator serves as the administrator's second-in-command and takes over in emergencies or when the administrator is absent.

The associate administrator is responsible for aviation safety and the assistant administrators are each responsible for one of the following areas: legal counsel, public affairs, civil rights, and government and industry.

The associate administrator for aviation safety is responsible for inspecting, supervising, and evaluating the National Airspace System for the purpose of expanding aviation safety. He or she serves as the administrator's safety representative to Congress, government agencies, and the aviation community. The associate administrator also establishes national safety policy, initiates special safety investigations, and reports on safety data compiled by the staff members.

The Office of Chief Counsel provides legal advice to the administrator for the handling of all legal matters concerning the FAA, including counsel as to the legality of the drafting and interpretation of FAA rules, regulations, and orders. The chief counsel deals with all legal claims by and against the FAA and oversees all legal proceedings before the courts, legislative committees, and government agencies.

The Office of Public Affairs is the primary voice of the FAA. This office coordinates the plans, programs, and up-to-date information that is presented to the public, aviation community, and news media.

The mission of the Office of Civil Rights is to advise the administrator on equal opportunity and civil rights matters within the FAA, including advice about the agency's employment practices and the services it offers to the public.

The Office of Government and Industry Affairs serves as the administrator's principal adviser on relations with Congress, the aviation industry, and government agencies. It promotes aviation by developing special programs to increase the FAA's involvement with the aviation community.

Each of the FAA's four executive directors oversees one of the following operations: policy, plans, and resource management; system operations; regulatory standards and compliance; and system development. These four areas encompass the most important day-to-day work of the FAA.

Policy, Plans, and Resource Management

This division manages the nine FAA regional offices and administrative entities such as the personnel office and the accounting office, encourages international

An FAA regional inspector examines the wing of an airplane. The nine FAA regional offices and the subordinate field offices provide flight standards inspection, certification, and maintenance services.

aviation, and oversees the Mike Monroney Aeronautical Center in Oklahoma City, Oklahoma.

The nine regional offices—Eastern, Central, Great Lakes, New England, Northwest Mountain, Southern, Southwest, Western-Pacific, and Alaskan—oversee the FAA field offices located throughout the United States and in Puerto Rico. The regional offices generally handle the operations of the agency—for example, the operation of air traffic services, certification of air personnel and airports, and installation of equipment. In other words, the administrator and his associate administrators make policies and issue regulations. These regulations are then put into effect through the regional and field offices. (This process has led to some regional differences and criticism from time to time, because the various field offices have often interpreted the regulations in different ways.)

An important policy and planning responsibility of the FAA's is dealing with foreign countries on air safety and air traffic control issues. The principal international agency for such problems is the International Civil Aviation Organization (ICAO), an agency of the United Nations—it has a membership of 157 countries—that is operated independently for the purpose of developing methods of international air navigation and transport and for the discussion of safety issues. For example, in 1983, after the Soviets had shot down an unarmed South Korean jetliner, the FAA worked hard and with some success to persuade the ICAO to condemn such an uncalled-for and violent reaction when the plane's crew was guilty of nothing more than bad navigation. The FAA also works closely with the ICAO on worldwide standards for navigation aids. For instance, it would not be wise for a Pan American plane approaching Moscow's airport not to be able to receive Soviet navigation signals because the guidance system was incompatible with the one Moscow was using. The FAA and the ICAO also consult on such legal matters as freedom to cross international borders and to land at any available airport in an emergency. (Because the United States was a pioneer in the development of both aircraft navigation systems and radio communications, English is the universal language of the skies.)

The Mike Monroney Aeronautical Center in Oklahoma City has two major functions: training air traffic controllers and conducting aeromedical research. Applicants for the job of air traffic controller must have four years of college or three years of general experience, and pass a medical examination, a security and background check, and a written aptitude test before entering the training program at the Monroney Center. Air traffic controllers must be no older than age 30 when entering on duty as a specialist at an airport traffic control tower

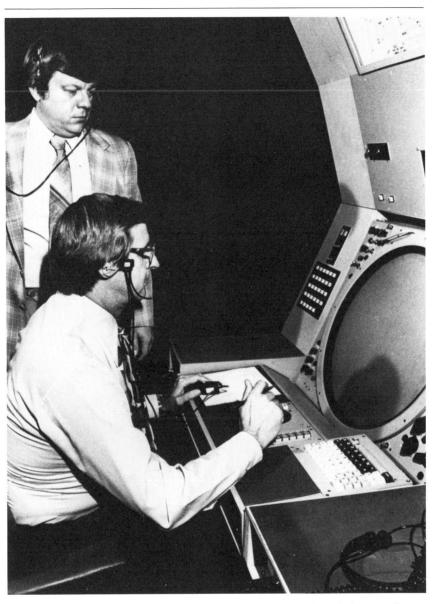

Two FAA instructors simulate an air traffic control training session at the FAA Academy in Oklahoma City, Oklahoma. Qualifications required for the job of air traffic controller include passing a written test, a personal interview, a medical examination, a security investigation, and completing the 10–12 week training program.

(terminal) or en route center. The length of training depends on the air traffic control field to be learned: Controllers training for en route centers take a 10-week course, and those training for air traffic control towers take a 12-week course. Flight service controllers have a three-month training period. The training program is divided between course work and facility training: Controllers learn in the classroom about FAA regulations and rules for handling air traffic, the characteristics of aircraft and aircraft performance, the mapping of airspace, and weather forecasting; the laboratory work involves simulated courses using radar and field work at an actual air traffic control facility.

The aeromedical research conducted at the Monroney Center includes such subjects as the effects of altitude, speed, vibration, temperature, noise, radiation, and drinking on pilot performance.

System Operations

This FAA division is responsible for four subordinate areas: air traffic, airway facilities, operations planning and policy, and operations resource management.

A team supervisor (left) discusses en route procedures with an air traffic controller. There are 24 en route centers, where controllers check on aircraft and issue instructions, clearances, and advice to pilots.

The single most important function the FAA performs is the management of airspace over the United States and its territories. As part of this duty, the FAA operates a network of 328 air traffic control towers (also called terminals), 24 air route traffic control centers (also called en route centers), and 275 flight service stations. The air traffic controllers at the towers handle air traffic into and out of airports. Air traffic controllers at the en route centers guide aircraft on the way to or from a tower (and into or out of airports not served by a terminal facility). Both towers and en route control centers deal with air traffic directly, through two-way radio communication networks that cover the entire United States. This means that a pilot flying in U.S. airspace is never out of range of an FAA radio station, day or night, 365 days a year. Usually several such stations are available to the pilot, to be used according to the kind of information that is needed.

To understand the duties of an FAA air traffic controller, one must understand that there are two sets of regulations under which a cross-country flight can be carried out; the degree of FAA air traffic control depends on which set of rules is applied to a flight. The first set of rules is known as visual flight rules (VFR). To fly under VFR, a pilot must be able to avoid collision with another aircraft or with obstructions on the ground by observing the hazards and by taking the necessary action—in other words, the pilot must always be able to "see and be seen" while in the air.

If, because of poor visibility, a pilot is unable to fly under VFR, he or she must fly under instrument flight rules (IFR). In this case, a radio beam is directed upward in a landing path from the approach end of a runway. The instruments in the aircraft then tell the pilot whether the plane is above, below, to the left, to the right, or precisely on course during landing procedures.

Flight service stations also serve as communication centers for pilots—primarily for private and business pilots who do not choose to enter the FAA's tightly controlled instrument flight rules system that requires almost constant radio communication with those pilots using it. The FAA provides route guidance to the pilot, allowing complete freedom from worry about flying into another airplane while under FAA guidance control. Pilots obtain information on the station's particular area, such as terrain, weather peculiarities, and any other information vital to the safety of a flight. Weather information is critical to the safety of flight, and the flight service stations do not wait for a pilot to ask about weather conditions; they provide a briefing automatically. If the station is visited personally by the pilot, current weather maps—also distributed by teletype—are available for inspection.

73

A flight service station specialist in Kankakee, Illinois, monitors the computer graphics system for changes in weather conditions. Flight service stations are descendants of the airways communications stations created in the 1920s to provide weather data to airmail service pilots. Today the staffed stations are being replaced with fully automated systems.

Flight service stations are located at most major airports used by private and business fliers, who are more likely to fly under visual flight rules. VFR requires little or no direct FAA control (except for airports having control towers) and considerably less radio communication. Flight service stations were once entirely staffed by controllers who accepted flight plans, both VFR and IFR, dispensed weather information and, when asked, offered a certain amount of advice about the routes and airports to be used by pilots. During the 1980s the staffed flight service station was being replaced by automated phone lines that enable pilots to file flight plans and obtain weather information. Automation has saved the FAA a considerable amount of money, but pilots miss the personal service available at the staffed stations and have fought the automation plan directly with the FAA and through the efforts of their congressmen. This has had the effect of delaying the FAA's conversion timetable, but year by year objections have been overcome and more flight service stations have been automated.

To keep order and maintain separation between aircraft, the FAA has established nearly 400,000 miles of designated federal airways. The FAA has designated more than 100,000 miles of jet routes above these airways, extending from 18,000 to 45,000 feet.

These airways are true highways of the sky, complete with their own electronic marker signs, access routes, directional guides, and even parking places—designated points around airports known to pilots as holding fixes. All kinds of air traffic—military, commercial, even private aircraft—can be ordered to hold at these racetrack-shaped parking areas in the sky so that air traffic controllers can bring arriving aircraft down to landings in an orderly way. Although the FAA controllers at times of bad weather make widespread use of these holding areas, the general rule of the agency is to keep aircraft waiting at departing airports until they can be cleared directly to a landing at their destinations. This policy saves fuel, reduces congestion in the air around busy airports, and makes for safer operations.

On some airlines passengers can listen to conversations between the pilot and the FAA controllers. First the pilot will talk to the ground controller, who will give permission for the "push back" from the boarding gate. Then the ground controller will clear the pilot to taxi to the active runway and will tell him or her if there is any delay in takeoff to be expected. Just before takeoff, the ground controller will "hand off" the flight—commercial airline planes are designated by their flight numbers, other aircraft by the FAA-assigned tail number—to the tower controller, who handles the takeoff.

As soon as the flight is airborne, the tower controller will hand off the flight to the departure controller, who in turn will hand off the flight to the FAA's en route center controller. As the flight progresses across the country, the pilot may be handed off to several such en route controllers before being handed off again to an arrival controller, and then to the tower at the arrival airport. When the aircraft lands, the ground controller takes over again.

In managing air traffic primarily through the use of radar, the FAA often has to deal with aircraft that suddenly appear on the radar screen. These aircraft are called "pop-ups." Sometimes controllers can communicate with these pop-up targets, particularly if the pilots have filed flight plans. But once in a

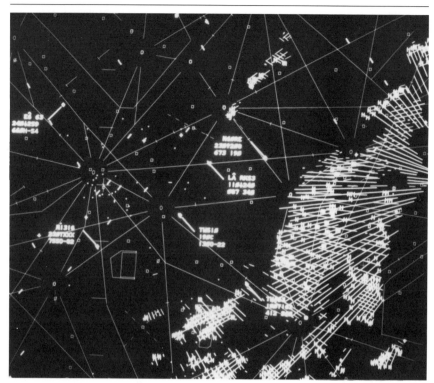

An air traffic controller's radar screen. When aircraft carry automatic altitude- and identity-reporting equipment, the controller's computer can take the information and display it on the screen next to the appropriate target, or blip. This data, which also includes the ground speed and flight number of the plane, begins to blink when the departure controller is ready to hand off the control of the flight to the en route center.

while the pop-ups turn out to be "unidentified flying objects" (UFOs). The U.S. Air Force is the organization that usually has to identify any UFO that is approaching the United States by air.

In addition to its roster of more than 16,000 air traffic controllers, the FAA also keeps a staff of several thousand service workers busy maintaining its complex system of visual and electronic navigation aids. Some of these are located on isolated mountaintops, and in the winter maintenance crews have to battle blizzards and hazardous roads in order to service them. Other aids, such as computers, require highly skilled electronics technicians to keep them operating. Because the FAA has had to continue to use old and obsolete radios

76

A visual navigation aid (top) guides pilots in the direction of an airport. A radar antenna (bottom) serves the Baltimore-Washington International Airport as an aid to aircraft. The FAA's Air Traffic Division, a part of System Operations, is responsible for the operation and maintenance of all navigation aids.

77

and computers—some of them powered by vacuum tubes that date back to World War II—its maintenance crews must also be specialists in repairing equipment that is out of date, with all the difficulties that arise when spare parts are no longer available.

Employees of System Operations also check the accuracy of the FAA's elaborate air-navigation beacon system, both in the United States and abroad. It is usual for the agency, after a major accident, to send out one or more inspection aircraft for the purpose of checking all the navigation aids ("navaids") that might have been used by any of the aircraft involved in the accident. Testimony that all of the navaids were operating properly and within allowed tolerances for error is an important piece of information for the National Transportation Safety Board when it conducts its investigation of the accident.

The Office of Operations Planning and Policy advises the executive director for System Operations and the administrator about the management of the National Airspace System, evaluates the efficiency and effectiveness of the system, and develops plans for air traffic and airway facilities.

The Office of Operations Resource Management directs the maintenance and operation of U.S. airspace, ensures that there are adequate monetary and human resources available to run the NAS plan, and provides the program to hire and train air traffic and airway facility employees.

Regulatory Standards and Compliance

This FAA division includes the offices of Regulation and Certification, Aviation Standards, and Program and Resource Management; the regional division managers who are responsible for flight standards, aircraft certification, security, and flight surgeons; the Aviation Standards National Field Office, which performs maintenance of FAA planes, flight inspections, and other regulatory functions located at the Aeronautical Center in Oklahoma City; and the overseas offices of Europe, Africa, and the Middle East headquartered in Brussels, Belgium.

In its role as a safety regulator, the FAA issues and enforces rules and regulations on standards to be used in manufacturing, maintaining, and operating aircraft. The agency also rates and certificates pilots and other air personnel (including aircraft mechanics), as well as airports that serve the airlines. At the more personal (as opposed to commercial) level the FAA issues experimental licenses for homebuilt planes. These must be either built or supervised by an FAA-licensed mechanic. Many are built from commercially designed and produced kits that have been approved by the FAA. Airline and

The Boeing 707, one of the first U.S. jet airliners, was put in service by Pan Am in 1958. The FAA issues and enforces regulations on the standards to be used in manufacturing aircraft.

other commercial pilots are often the people who build these small planes at home. Both the building and later use of these planes satisfies many pilots' love of flying in a way that flying a large plane along a commercial air route can never do.

Pilots of the smallest of these personal planes, the so-called ultralights, are not even required to hold an FAA pilot's license. This is also true of glider pilots, who are also not required to pass a medical examination. For this reason, many pilots who have minor medical problems often take up glider flying.

In addition to holding a current license, graduated according to the pilot's level of proficiency—student, private, commercial, or commercial with an air transport rating—all pilots (except ultralight and glider pilots) must also hold a current medical certificate. To be a pilot obviously requires the ability to see and hear reasonably well (even pilots flying the biggest jetliners are allowed to

A commercial airline pilot must pass stringent proficiency tests as well as a medical examination before obtaining an FAA license to fly.

wear glasses). Pilots with heart problems or such medical problems as the more serious forms of diabetes are usually denied a medical certificate.

The medical examinations for pilots are given by private doctors who have taken FAA courses, passed an FAA examination, and are certified to give such examinations by the FAA. Airlines usually hire their own doctors to give their pilots medical examinations, not only to award FAA medical licenses but also to advise any pilots who might have personal medical problems. Alcoholism, even drug abuse, is not unknown among pilots, and early counseling can often head off trouble for both the afflicted pilot and his or her employers.

If a pilot is so foolish as to drink while flying the FAA can suspend or revoke his or her license. But such cases are difficult to prove, because the FAA does not require pilots suspected of drinking to take any kind of test for alcohol consumption, such as the breathalizer tests commonly used by local and state law enforcement officers when a motorist is suspected of driving while intoxicated. Pilots who are killed in air crashes, at least those that are investigated by the National Transportation Safety Board (NTSB), are routinely given alcohol blood tests by the local coroner's office. It took a federal law before this requirement could be put into effect nationally because subjecting a dead body to tests is governed by local laws that often are written to protect the sanctity of the dead.

Although the FAA investigates accidents involving small planes (and often takes disciplinary action—a letter of admonition or a small fine—against pilots who are involved in accidents), it does so only on delegation from the NTSB. The job of the NTSB is to examine the accidents of public carriers, including air, rail, highway, and pipeline accidents. (Although accidents involving private automobiles are exempt from its authority, during the early 1980s the NTSB conducted a public campaign to persuade states to pass laws requiring motorists to use approved safety seats when carrying small children.) Any air accident that involves a fatality or substantial property damage is investigated by the NTSB itself, almost always with the help of the FAA. After an investigation, the NTSB makes a formal finding of probable cause; if no cause can be determined, the case is kept open for any additional evidence that might show up later.

Not infrequently, the FAA itself is declared a "causal factor" in an air accident. Air traffic controllers can, of course, cause accidents as well as prevent them. On one occasion, a controller working heavy traffic in bad

Pilots of ultralights are not required to hold an FAA pilot's license.

This commercial jetliner crashed after its tires blew out during take-off at Los Angeles International Airport in 1978. The National Transportation Safety Board investigated the accident, in which two people were killed, and recommended that the FAA set limits on taxiing distances and speeds and improve standards for retreaded tires.

weather directed an airliner into the side of a mountain. In a number of cases controllers have cleared airplanes too close to one another, causing what is commonly known as a "near miss." Air accidents almost always result in lawsuits for civil damages, and the FAA quietly pays up when one of its employees is found to be at fault.

The FAA publishes the *Federal Air Regulations* and keeps them up-to-date so pilots will know the rules and regulations they are required to follow; a host of additional bits and pieces of information must constantly be provided to pilots. A simple matter of closing down a navigation aid for a short period while it is being repaired can become a life-and-death issue for a pilot flying in stormy weather. Information of this kind is sent out in the form of "notices to airmen"—"notams" for short. Notams are available immediately to pilots who confer with the FAA's flight service stations because they have been received by teletype within minutes after being issued.

A lesser-known but important function performed by the FAA within the Division of Regulatory Standards and Compliance is providing a register where ownership of aircraft can be recorded in the same way real estate can be recorded in municipal or county courthouses. Along with the recording of aircraft ownership titles, the FAA also records ownership of aircraft engines, propellers, accessories, and spare parts.

In addition to licensing airports used by the airlines, the FAA administers a federal subsidy program that amounts to more than $1 billion a year. As a part of this job, the FAA considers the environmental impact of airports on their surrounding community, particularly in terms of noise and air pollution. The FAA also develops and publishes standards and technical guidance on airport planning, design, safety, and operations, and it provides federal grant money to help local airport authorities and other public agencies produce master plans for airports and for airport improvements such as new or larger runways.

For many years the FAA was also responsible for funding two of its own airports: Washington National and Dulles International airports in Washington, D.C. However, the FAA was never comfortable dealing with local pressures and politicians while it ran Dulles and National, and finally, under President

A cabin attendant explains the safety equipment—seat belts, flotation devices, and oxygen masks—and points out the various emergency exits available to passengers. The FAA requires all airlines to give this safety information to their passengers before takeoff.

Ronald Reagan and Transportation Secretary Elizabeth Dole, control of the two airports was transferred by act of Congress in 1987 to a local operating group. All of the FAA's employees at the two airports were transferred to the new airport authority.

System Development

This division of the FAA organization directs research in the development of airports, aircraft design, and aviation equipment.

As part of a continuous effort to upgrade its facilities and equipment to meet the ever-increasing volume of air traffic, the FAA conducts research, engineering, and development work at its principal technical center, located near Atlantic City, New Jersey. For example, before the new computers were installed in the FAA's en route traffic control centers during the late 1980s, they had first to be tested in simulated traffic control situations at the technical center in a six-month operation designed to make sure that when controllers are plugged into the new computers there is no malfunction that could jeopardize air safety. Engines, radios, navigation transmitters, receivers—

Dulles International Airport in Washington, D.C., was designed by the award-winning architect Eero Saarinen in 1950. The FAA was responsible for the operation and funding of the airport until Congress transferred its operations to a local authority in 1987.

An FAA display-panel technician checks the high voltage section on a computer readout terminal at an en route center. The FAA continues to upgrade its air traffic facilities and equipment by researching new computer systems at the FAA Technical Center, located near Atlantic City, New Jersey.

everything of a mechanical or electronic nature, in the air and on the ground— gets tested at the technical center at one time or another.

The System Development Division also includes the FAA's National Airspace System (NAS) plan for purchasing new computers and other equipment, improving airport radar systems, and building new runways.

An air traffic control specialist peers out from the glass-walled room at the top of the control tower at Washington National Airport. The FAA estimates that by 1995 there will be more than 74 million flight operations at airports equipped with towers.

FIVE

The FAA
Tomorrow

As air traffic continues to grow, the FAA's job gets more difficult, and it will probably continue to be demanding in the foreseeable future. By the time the FAA completes its National Airspace System plan in the early 1990s, much of the $12 billion in equipment now being put in place may already be obsolete. Like Alice in *Alice's Adventures in Wonderland,* the FAA has to keep running just to stay in place as technology grows and improves.

In April 1988 a seven-member aviation safety commission, established by an act of Congress and appointed by President Ronald Reagan, recommended that the FAA be made an independent agency with a new safety chief to supervise the regulation of the airline industry. The commission's report said that the regulatory system had to be modified to accommodate the new aircraft technology, "to respond to heightened sensitivity on the part of the public to aviation safety, and to act on the backlog of potentially worthwhile safety improvements that have been languishing because of diffused authority and accountability." The commission recommended that the FAA be removed from the DOT's jurisdiction so that it would have more power. In its report to the president, the commission proposed that a nine-member board of governors—appointed by the president and confirmed by the Senate—oversee the FAA. An administrator would be chosen for a seven-year term to manage the agency, and a director of aviation safety, also selected for a seven-year term, would oversee the regulatory functions of the agency. The commission also recommended that the agency should be free from civil service rules so that it could attract the best people to top-level positions and could pay employees enough to accept posts in cities with higher costs of living. Other proposed changes submitted by the commission were

1. Institute a national rather than a regional certification program for the major air carriers.

2. Establish a nationwide program of surprise inspections where air carriers would have no advance notice as they do at present.

3. Increase the number of inspectors and have priority inspections for those carriers undergoing major changes.

4. Reduce the differences in standards for planes and in operating procedures between commuter lines and large national carriers.

5. Require all aircraft to be equipped with a transponder (a special radio that emits a signal) that shows air traffic controllers the altitude of the plane on radar.

6. Base certification of airports on their passenger volumes and not on the types of equipment they have.

7. Change the FAA rule-making procedures so that it will have explicit accountability for air safety.

Although the commission's recommendations had the support of many members of Congress, most top officials in the executive branch and in Congress believed it highly unlikely that legislation to remove the FAA from the DOT could be passed in an election year.

In August 1988 the FAA went ahead on its own initiative and restructured its administrative organization. The 23 positions of assistant administrator—these officials had been responsible for divisions such as air traffic, personnel, public affairs, and airports, and reported directly to the administrator—were consolidated into 4 positions with the title of executive director. The FAA's plan was to provide continuity in the philosophy of its middle management and to give the executive directors more responsibility in the decision-making process, increasing the likelihood that they would stay at the FAA for a longer period of time. Prior to the reorganization, the assistant directors rarely remained for more than a year.

As the airlines continue to agitate for transfer of the FAA away from the DOT, congressional leaders are hopeful that legislation will be forthcoming that

The cockpit of the McDonnell Douglas MD-80 jet. A new wind shear detection system—approved by the FAA—will provide warning data for such advanced airliners in the early 1990s.

will return the FAA to its former status as an independent agency, reporting directly to the president. The FAA has an important impact on all air travelers—a group of people that now makes up a majority of the U.S. population—and the battle for FAA independence is of interest to all Americans.

The steady increase in the number of Americans who travel by air has not come as a total surprise to the FAA. Each year the agency's planners prepare a forecast of air traffic covering as much as 10 years ahead. The FAA estimates that by 1995, 1,700,000 people will board U.S. airlines everyday. Generally the FAA's forecasts are accurate. What the FAA has not been able to forecast is the continuing effect on the airlines of deregulation, which makes it possible for anyone with sufficient money to form an airline with routes to fly almost anywhere in the United States.

An airplane lands at night at Chicago's O'Hare International Airport—one of the busiest airports in the United States. In October 1988 the FAA, worried by a series of mistakes made by air traffic controllers, cut peak-hour (5:00 P.M. to 8:00 P.M.) landings at O'Hare from 96 to 80 landings per hour.

Because of the increase in air traffic, there are some airports where a new airline cannot fly at the peak hours most attractive to travelers. At these airports the FAA operates a "slot control" program that gives the existing carriers priority over new entrants in flying into and out of the airport. In addition to rationing access to airports, the FAA takes a direct interest in other factors that might handicap new entrants. These include allocation of ticket counters and boarding gates within the terminals.

The rash of airline mergers that followed deregulation also caused problems for the FAA. When airlines consolidated, they tended to bunch even more flights at hub airports, and the FAA could do little or nothing about it. The airlines took the brunt of the anger caused by the resulting delays, but wherever possible they tried to put the blame on the FAA. Continuing delays and passenger frustration could well prompt Congress to take some action in an effort to remove the FAA from the DOT. But no matter which way Congress decides to go in the future, the FAA will continue to operate very much in the same way it always has: directly controlling air traffic, testing and licensing pilots and airplanes alike, and trying hard to keep up with the ever-increasing flow of air traffic.

Federal Aviation Administration
Department of Transportation

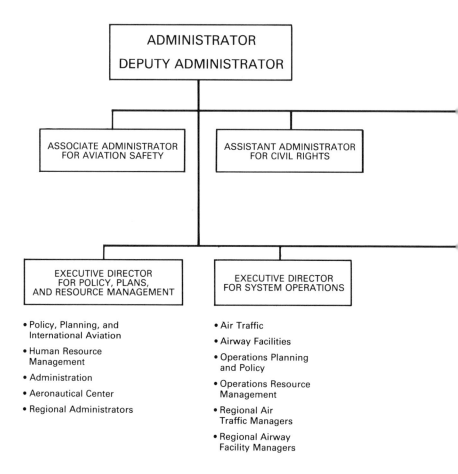

ADMINISTRATOR

DEPUTY ADMINISTRATOR

ASSOCIATE ADMINISTRATOR
FOR AVIATION SAFETY

ASSISTANT ADMINISTRATOR
FOR CIVIL RIGHTS

EXECUTIVE DIRECTOR
FOR POLICY, PLANS,
AND RESOURCE MANAGEMENT

EXECUTIVE DIRECTOR
FOR SYSTEM OPERATIONS

- Policy, Planning, and
  International Aviation
- Human Resource
  Management
- Administration
- Aeronautical Center
- Regional Administrators

- Air Traffic
- Airway Facilities
- Operations Planning
  and Policy
- Operations Resource
  Management
- Regional Air
  Traffic Managers
- Regional Airway
  Facility Managers

| CHIEF COUNSEL | ASSISTANT ADMINISTRATOR FOR GOVERNMENT AND INDUSTRY | ASSISTANT ADMINISTRATOR FOR PUBLIC AFFAIRS |

• Regional Counsels

| EXECUTIVE DIRECTOR FOR REGULATORY STANDARDS AND COMPLIANCE | EXECUTIVE DIRECTOR FOR SYSTEM DEVELOPMENT |

- • Regulation
  and Certification

- • Aviation Standards

- • Program and
  Resource Management

- • Regional Division
  Managers

  —Flight Standards

  —Aircraft Certification

  —Security

  —Flight Surgeons

  —Aviation Standards
  National Field Office

- • Advanced Design
  and Management Control

- • National Airspace
  System Development

- • Airports

- • Technical Center

- • Regional Airport
  Managers

GLOSSARY

Aeronautics   A science that deals with flight and operation of aircraft.

Air traffic controller   One who directs the arrival and departure of airplanes and uses radar to monitor their movements throughout their course of flight.

Barnstormer   One who flies an airplane, usually through rural districts, and performs stunts or takes passengers on sight-seeing tours.

Crop duster   One who sprays crops with fungicidal or insecticidal dusts from a plane.

Deregulation   The process of removing restrictions and regulations, allowing for increased competition within an industry.

Dogfighting   Combat between two or more fighter planes, usually at close range.

Doppler radar system   A system that measures velocity and is used to determine wind conditions.

En route center   A station used to guide aircraft on the way to or from an air traffic control tower at an airport.

Flight service station   Communication center that distributes weather information and is used primarily by private and business pilots not flying under the FAA's instrument flight rules.

Hub airport   An airport designated as the center of operations for an airline. The airline's flights originate from and return to the hub airport.

Instrument flight rules   Navigation of an airplane by instruments only; used in conditions of poor visibility.

Near miss   A situation in which controllers clear airplanes for takeoff or landing too close to one another and they nearly collide.

Notams   Notices to airmen that contain such information as the condition of a navigation aid along a particular flight course.

Pop-ups   Unidentified objects or aircraft that appear suddenly on an air traffic controller's radar screen.

Reconnaissance   An exploratory military survey of enemy territory.

Rumrunner   One who used an airplane, or other means of transport, to smuggle alcohol into the United States during Prohibition.

Supersonic transport   A commercial transport plane that can fly faster than the speed of sound.

Transponder   A radio or radar system that emits a signal and is used to detect, identify, and locate objects.

Ultralight   A small lightweight plane used for private flights.

Visual flight rules   Navigation system which requires that a pilot must always be able to see and be seen while in the air in order to avoid danger.

Wind-shear   An extreme shift in wind speed and direction that can abruptly stop the normal lift-producing flow of air over a plane's wings; often the cause of plane crashes.

Wing walker   One who performs stunts in the air while attached to the wing of a plane.

SELECTED REFERENCES

Burkhardt, Robert. *The Federal Aviation Administration.* New York: Praeger, 1967.

Burnham, Frank. *Cleared to Land: The FAA Story.* Fallbrook, CA: Aero Publishers, 1977.

Christy, Joe. *High Adventure: The First 75 Years of Civil Aviation.* Blue Ridge Summit, PA: TAB Books, 1985.

Federal Aviation Administration. *FAA Historical Fact Book: A Chronology 1926–1971.* Washington, D.C.: U.S. Government Printing Office, 1974.

———. Annual Reports. Issued yearly for the years 1959–1966. Washington, D.C.: U.S. Government Printing Office.

Halaby, Najeeb E. *Crosswinds: An Airman's Memoir.* Garden City, NY: Doubleday, 1978.

Horwitch, Mel. *Clipped Wings: The American SST Conflict.* Cambridge, MA: M.I.T. Press, 1982.

Kent, Richard J. *Safe, Separated, and Soaring: A History of Federal Civil Aviation Policy, 1961–1972.* Washington, D.C.: U.S. Government Printing Office, 1980.

Komons, Nick A. *Bonfires to Beacons: Federal Civil Aviation Policy Under the Air Commerce Act, 1926–1938.* Washington, DC: U.S. Government Printing Office, 1978.

O'Neil, Paul. *Barnstormers and Speed Kings.* Alexandria, VA: Time-Life, 1981.

Redford, Emmette S. *Congress Passes the Federal Aviation Act of 1958.* University: University of Alabama Press, 1961.

Rhyne, Charles S. *The Civil Aeronautics Act Annotated.* Washington, DC: National Law Book Company, 1939.

Rochester, Stuart I. *Takeoff at Mid-Century: Federal Civil Aviation Policy in the Eisenhower Years, 1953–1961.* Washington, DC: U.S. Government Printing Office, 1976.

Whitnah, Donald. *Safer Skyways: Federal Control of Aviation, 1926–1966.* Ames: Iowa State University Press, 1967.

Wilson, John R. M. *Turbulence Aloft: The Civil Aeronautics Administration Amid Wars and Rumors of Wars, 1938–1953.* Washington, DC: U.S. Government Printing Office, 1979.

Witkin, Richard. "Powerful New Role is Urged for the FAA on Airline Safety." *New York Times,* April 19, 1988, 1.

INDEX

Eisenhower, Dwight D., 22, 23, 50, 51
Engen, Donald D., 62, 64–65

Federal Air Regulations, 82
Federal Aviation Administration (FAA)
  Airline Deregulation Act (1978) and, 55–57
  airport security and, 57–58
  air traffic controllers' strike and, 59–62
  creation of, 52
  drug smuggling and, 57–59
  Federal Air Regulations, 82
  future role, 87–91
  history of, 15–23
  licensing of pilots, 78–80
  Office of Chief Counsel, 68
  Office of Civil Rights, 68–69
  Office of Government and Industry Affairs, 69
  Office of Public Affairs, 68
  pilot certification, 78–80
  Policy, Plans and Resource Management Division, 69–72
  proposed changes in, 88
  regional offices, 70
  Regulatory Standards and Compliance Division, 78–84
  role of, 15, 23, 67–68
  safety inspection program 62–64
  service workers, 76–78
  structure of, 68–85
  supersonic transport program, 52–55
  Systems Development Division, 84–85
  Systems Operations Division, 72–78
  Technical Center, Atlantic City, 84–85

Federal Aviation Agency (FAA), 51–52
Flight communications service, 49
Flight service stations, 74
France, 55

Governmental agencies, U.S. *See specific agencies*
Great Britain, 55
Greece, 58

Halaby, Najeeb E., 23
Helms, Lynn, 61
Henderson, Paul, 35
Hoover, Herbert, 36, 39, 41
Hub airports, 56–57

Instrument flight rules, 73–74
International Civil Aviation Organization (ICAO), 49–50, 70
Interstate Commerce Commission, 20
Italo-Turkish War, 27
Italy, 26–27, 57

Johnson, Lyndon, 52

Kelly Air Mail Act (1925), 20, 35, 36
Kelly, Clyde, 36

Leonardo da Vinci International Airport, Rome, 57
Lewis, Drew, 59, 61
Licensing of pilots, 78–80
Lindbergh, Charles A., 24, 31, 39
Lockheed, 54

McArtor, T. Allan, 65
MacCracken, William P., Jr., 34, 36, 39

Robert Burkhardt, author, reporter, and licensed pilot, has written on aviation for such periodicals as the *Journal of Commerce, Flying Magazine, Airline Executive, The Economist,* and *The Aeroplane.* Formerly editor and publisher of *Air Cargo* magazine and transport editor of *Aviation Daily,* he has also written two books, *The Civil Aeronautics Board* and *The Federal Aviation Administration,* and is currently working on a book about air safety.

Arthur M. Schlesinger, jr., served in the White House as special assistant to Presidents Kennedy and Johnson. He is the author of numerous acclaimed works in American history and has twice been awarded the Pulitzer Prize. He taught history at Harvard College for many years and is currently Albert Schweitzer Professor of the Humanities at the City College of New York.

PICTURE CREDITS: